THE WHOLE DAMN VALLEY
VOICES FROM THE METHOW

By Diana Hottell

Diana Hottell

The Whole Damn Valley – Voices of the Methow

Published 2007 by Shafer Historical Museum, Winthrop, Washington
ISBN 978-0-9779726-1-6

Credits
Except for the Clara Williams eulogy, the content of this book has been rewritten from material first published in The Methow Valley News, Wenatchee World, Goat Wall Street Journal, the Seattle Weekly and Country Side Magazine. Permission to use photographs was granted by the Methow Valley News and the Wenatchee World.

Photographers: Diana Hottell, Bill Hottell, Floyd Luke, Mike Irwin and Tim Patrick.
Edited by Karen West
Design by Sally Ranzau
Cover painting: *Outbuilding at the Lloyd Ranch* ©2007 Mary Powell, oil on canvas

Printed in the USA

Acknowledgements

The Shafer Historical Museum Board of Directors wishes to thank Diana Hottell for the gift of her manuscript. The museum will receive all proceeds from the sale of this book.

Dedication

To all those who call the Methow Valley home, past, present and to come. Also to Bill, who had the foresight to have been born in this part of the state and to bring me to my life here.

Introduction

I once asked Edna Darwood, one of the first white children born in the Methow Valley, what had drawn her parents here in 1894. As she opened her mouth to reply, her husband Stanley answered out of turn.

"The whole damn valley was here!" he bellowed. "That's what was here!"

It took me a dozen years to figure out what he meant. The reason I did is that the valley started disappearing – at least the part I believe Stanley meant by "the whole damn valley."

I spent those years in this fold of Cascade Mountains in Washington State asking questions and putting people's stories in local newspapers. I wrote from week to week, hoping to get facts straight, knowing each person had to live with what was printed.

Written between 1976 and 1987, those stories caught people in the act of coming to grips with whatever fate dealt out to them. Although I listened to tales I swore never to divulge, much of what was told me was offered in the hopes I could make some sense of whole lifetimes. And I seethed with opinions about what I heard and saw.

I remember in particular one farmer's mourning for the valley he had once known. He had been away for years. As he drove past fields once tended with devotion and understanding, his eyes grew cold as Davis Lake in winter. The land had gone to weed. Farm machinery rusted, barns slumped.

Then came the dying. Season upon season, a good number of pioneers passed into Upper Pastures, leaving an emptiness I felt was never going to be filled again. I noticed it first in a video store. People were intent on the film for that evening, not on crops they'd just seeded. Nobody seemed particularly grounded.

Realtors' signs were tacked to so many fence posts one wondered if anyone wanted to stick around.

This book is full of stories of good people doing good things for each other. It's a hopeful read in disparaging times. Just to have this material in one place, to delight in, I gathered it together, tampered with it a little, and offer it as a tribute to a time that's kissed us goodbye.

Maybe, too, this is my way of expiating a guilt. When I moved here I bought a farm and never farmed it. Grass devoured irises and raspberries planted in such painstaking profusion around the house. I tried to stop that killing grass, but my efforts weren't good enough. I didn't have the knack.

Instead, I wrote about the people who had the knack, people who knew effort to the very depths of their beings.

I'm not out for more accolades for these stories. I've gotten all the mileage I deserve from them already. One woman I approached at first had been reluctant to talk to me because she felt what she had to say wasn't interesting. However, when she read the finished piece, she looked up from the pages in quiet astonishment. "My life really was interesting, wasn't it?" she said.

I've carried that exclamation around as my reward since then.

This collection, then, is my small contribution to the memory of this whole damn valley.

Diana Hottell, 1995

Chapter 1

Eighteen Characters from a Cast of Thousands

Bill Robler was talking to two Indians.

"Felix," he said, "I've heard that you people are good at predicting how the winter's going to be. What's it going to be like this winter?

Felix answered, "Oh, it's going to be a hard one, very hard."

The other Indian said, "No, it's going to be an easy winter."

Bill scratched his head. "Well, what is this? One of you says it's going to be hard and the other says it's not."

And Felix responded, "Oh, I got hay to sell, and he got no hay to sell."

Necessity often posed as the common denominator in directing lives in the Methow Valley. However, more recent residents are moved by a number of different motives, including the need to escape from a dehumanizing world.

Hollywood movie actress Stella Stevens bought a ranch up Libby Creek back in the '70s. The kind of elation she expresses hits almost anyone who settles for any length of time in the land drained by the Methow River and its many tributaries.

"When I moved to Chicamun Creek Ranch," Stella said, "I laughed aloud. I felt like I'd stolen something. THEY weren't able to stop me! It was the only dream not stolen, used or killed. No one is conning me here. No one kowtows to me. In Palm Springs or Los Angeles I'm always dealing with people who are out for my money. I felt as if I had a hole eaten through my stomach. I was made physically ill by the conning. Boy, is it a relief not to feel like a target anymore. I don't feel as if my energies are being wasted here at the ranch. When I tear down a fence, paint a room, that's for my own enjoyment. No one can take that enjoyment from me. In Hollywood my talents are wasted. I think my life here is more interesting than any character I've ever played."

Charlie and the Antlers

Charlie Schmidt, left of piano, playing spoons at The Antlers Tavern 1975

The bones of our spoons player, Charlie Schmidt, were laid to rest this afternoon up at Beaver Creek Cemetery. It's raining this evening, damping down the wounded grass around his grave. The light's gloomy and I'm alone, ready to tell the story about playing music at the Antlers Tavern in Twisp for 15 years.

The band won't be the same without Charlie. We'd grown attached to the clack and tocking of those utensils and especially to his cocked smile ready to go off every time you met his eye.

No more will Bill lean east on his beer keg and say, "Hey, Charlie! 'Alabama Jubilee' in B flat. Tune 'em up!" No more will Charlie shoot a glance over his can of Heidelberg balanced on the upright or rattle his snappy spoons between thigh and the few fingers that remained on his hand.

A word about the band: the greying diddlybopper behind the four-string plectrum banjo is me, the spy imperfectly hidden by the short-neck instrument. I'm married to the guy slamming the ivories. The blurred arm thwacking the parachute cord attached to the oil drum belongs to gutbucketer Dan Doran. Bob Spiwak blows into a clarinet but prefers belting out the lyrics.

Yeah, we're a motley assortment, and we're local color.

Gritty racks of antlers and scruffy game heads jut from the cinder block walls, high up, over beer posters, framed photos of the tavern 50 years ago, a few dollar bills tacked to a board. A gallon jar festers with pickled eggs. The jukebox sports an Hawaiian girl who's been cavorting with enormous chrysanthemums for as long as I can remember. Pocked with caulk marks, the oily floor is etched with the legible graffiti of past scuffles.

Two weeks after moving to this remoteness, Bill and I pushed through that tavern door, sat in the dim afternoon sunshine oozing through the greasy windows, played a few tunes, and got hired for the night. Since then, we've gone through several bosses, a shooting, and brawls conducted in the finest Western style.

Charlie joined us right off the bat. Little by little, music makers took their places as if pre-ordained and stuck around for years.

We never bother to practice. Besides, sometimes on a dead night the few customers rest their heads slap in the middle of their water rings, or else get so engrossed in their own arguments they pay little attention to whether or not we forgot the verse to "Georgia," or if the sax player, to kill the monotony, cuts up by blowing every note a quarter tone off.

If it came right down to it, we'd pay to play there. There are nights when I kick into some other plane, made up entirely of music. I float on waves of nearly impermissible pleasure when I know it's the only force on earth.

Those times, the feed store owner leaps up to dance with the postmaster's wife; Ron and Sue tell you, for the sixth time this year, it's their anniversary; Joe free-falls from the bouncy dance floor (big as a bedspread); Darlene, ruffling Bill's hair (which he hates), keeps keening the words to every song; dancers trip over our shoes and we recoil instinctively, then smile and right our drinks.

With uncommon graciousness, our audience habitually forgives us our trespasses. No one's complained because we haven't varied our repertoire, and people consistently forgive us our episodic zaniness when we spangle the smoke-blue air with random notes.

On the surface of things, it looks as if we're just playing "When You Wore a Tulip," but we're also wondering why so-and-so is out with whosiwhatsis, or we're unconsciously tallying the trials or triumphs or mis-moves of everyone who sweeps through the swinging door. Private facts are public domain; everyone's up for scrutiny, including ourselves. But they exonerate us and buy us a round, just as we forgive them and draw them onto the dance floor with a particularly silky rendition of "Dream," with Bob crooning into his low-powered mike.

Some nights, usually in winter, there's not a strange face in the bunch. It's a private party. But then there are evenings when the moon is full to bursting, when violence is as palpable as the glutinous smoke that passes for air in the place. Those nights have proved diverting, to put it blandly. Oh, I could tell you stories, but that would be jumping the gun.

Anyway, here I am at home tonight, watching the rain fall, reflecting on music and death. I haven't winterkilled yet, but Matt's back in Montana playing his banjo for his mustangs, and Wayne's away in Oregon coaxing more genteel tunes from his clarinet.

But Charlie, now, he's gone for good.

I went to see him today, lying in that coffin of his down at Precht's Chapel. I must say, he didn't quite look himself; he looked more as if life had finally gotten to be too much for him.

But I've got to tell you. Clasped in those depleted hands of his were his spoons, the very ones he'd wound with adhesive tape so he wouldn't get blisters playing as hard as he did.

Since they play Dixieland in Heaven, Charlie's in full swing now, the newest member of God's Holy Ragtime Band. I can hear him now, popping those things so that all our departed friends and relatives in the Pearly Afterglow can't restrain themselves from dancing on air.

(July 1987)

A Mining Grandmother

Susie Klinkert and her co-pilot Boots

Gunning Big Red toward the mountain dead ahead, the 65-year-old grandmother spit gravel like bullets from the three fat tires. Her co-pilot's ears flapped madly against the back of his neck.

Susie Klinkert, by her own admission, has always been somewhat unorthodox. Her co-pilot, a cockapoo named Boots, could care less about that; he has a ball riding shotgun on Susie's Honda three-wheeler. This is Susie's territory – at the absolute end of the Twisp River Road, miles beyond the last habitation.

Passing the dilapidated cabin in the ghost settlement of Gilbert where she spent her honeymoon in 1940, she shouted above her machine's din, "I tell people if they didn't honeymoon with a box of dynamite under their bed, they haven't lived. Actually, I've spent more than half my life sleeping over dynamite. That's the best place for it, by the way."

Widowed after 45 years of marriage to her powderman and gold miner husband Johnny Klinkert, Susie is on the mend.

"I get too much mileage out of life to just shut the door and close the curtains," she said, pulling up to her clapboard cabin beside a diverted tributary of North Creek. "So many options are available for a widow. I never would have thought it possible."

Susie has a home in Twisp, 25 miles back down the road, but much of the summer season Susie's at the cabin near her gold mine claims.

When Johnny died suddenly in 1985, Forest Service officials hoped Susie would give up her many mining claims, since they're situated in the recently formed Chelan-Sawtooth Wilderness area.

But Susie being Susie, she defied expectations and filed assessment.

"It's every miner's hope to strike it rich," Susie said. "It was Johnny's dream and now it's mine." She rolled freshly picked huckleberries from a towel into plastic containers for later use in muffins and pancakes. "But everyone knows," she continued, "that in mining, as in love, the romance is in the chase. It's the prospecting that counts."

Since Johnny's death, Susie has hung pretty curtains on a few of the cabin windows and covered two walls with her mother's religious tapestries.

"I've feminized the place," she admitted. "I keep expecting Johnny to hurl thunderbolts."

She laughed and wiped her eyes.

"God, I miss him," she said. "But it's OK. My cup is more than half full. Don't get me wrong, he was no saint. But 40 out of 45 years we were married were great."

Just outside the windows leap the Cascades, the same mountains that hold the gold Johnny never laid his hands on.

Searching for gold is still in Susie's blood, but meanwhile, she finds treasure where she can, in her children and grandchildren, the loaded huckleberry bushes, her new future. Filing assessment on her gold claims keeps Johnny's dreams alive. She may even file claims elsewhere.

She's up for it. Just ask Boots.

(July 1987)

The Blur at the Slaughterhouse

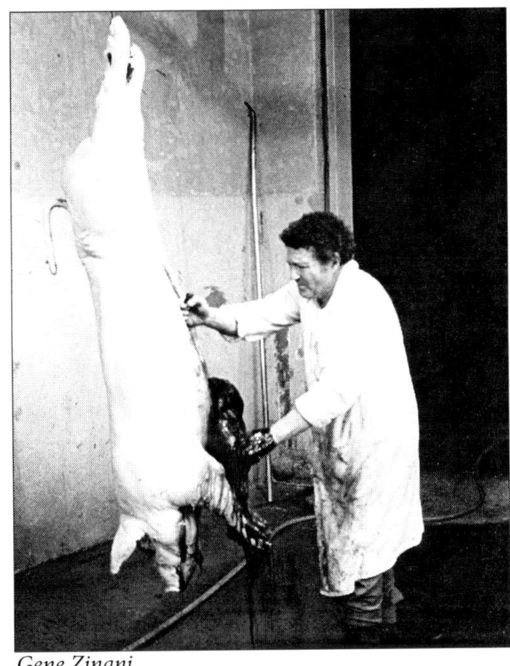

Gene Zinani

The man is fast. He walks fast, works fast, talks fast. And he's good.

An expert is a joy to behold when he's in gear. Just because Gene Zinani happens to be in the business of killing, skinning, and cutting animals doesn't make his actions with the knife any less beautiful than, say, a welder's expertise with a torch or a carpenter's handling of a saw.

When Gene goes to work, often at 4 a.m., there's no slack time. Unless you're on your toes it's hard to keep the man in focus. He works a blue streak whether he's scraping hair off a scalded pig, gutting a steer, skinning a lamb, slicing roasts from a hanging quarter, or setting a smoky fire of applewood under bacon and hams.

He expects his assistants to do the same. His son Geno, not long out of Liberty Bell High, is learning the business from the killing chute to the band saw. Marti Hough, an eight year veteran of the original slaughterhouse, was dragged out of retirement to do the wrapping. Harriet, Gene's wife of seven months, who in real life is the head administrator at the county's District Court, works beside him on the weekends.

This flurry doesn't mean that the good times don't roll, too, at Methow Valley's only slaughterhouse. (Not that the cows two-step down the chute.)

"We have a lot of fun," Gene often says. He likes razzing his favorite customers, he's loud with his jokes, and if you want to get into verbal combat just engage him in some thoughts about the state game department.

One day last week Gene said he was thinking about that sector of the government. His eyes flashed as he wielded his knife even faster on the beef rump. He slammed his sharp cutting instrument down on the marble counter, strode full tilt down the corridor to the hanging cooler, yanked a denuded beast off the hook and displayed the pathetic specimen: a 35 pound deer.

"This is thanks to the game department for giving a Great White Hunter from the coast a license to come over here and kill our little fawns!" Spitting mad that such killing goes on, he threw it back up onto its hook and slammed the heavy door on the sight.

"Take the ears off that deer," Marti added, "it would look like a squirrel."

Gene doesn't condemn hunting. In fact, he likes to see big bucks come through the slaughterhouse door, ones that have been carefully handled by those who know how to keep the meat from souring.

Gene knows meat. He can appraise an animal on the spot and is quick to compliment the owner of a healthy animal.

Gene took over the Twisp establishment from Emery Halterman in 1975 "on a handshake," closed up his slaughterhouse in California and brought his family to the valley.

"Been here struggling ever since," he grins. "Actually, it's wonderful here. I wouldn't go back to that country for anything."

I visited Gene the day he butchered a load of hogs. The concrete high-ceilinged slaughter room looked like a ring of hell with hooks and saws and knives and a cauldron steaming. The ungodly noise of the scraper that de-hairs the scalded pigs, mixed with sticky blood underfoot, set a scene not meant for the squeamish or the vegetarian.

I was there for less than an hour. In that time Gene and Geno had killed (with one swift .22 bullet to each brain), stuck, scalded, scraped, cut and hung nine huge porkers.

Hoses constantly water-swept the floors and animals. Then they were done, hanging there in the eerie light, and they were done perfectly.

At one point when Gene's arms were deep inside a sow's body undoing guts from the meat, blood flowing freely, he said, "People ask me all the time how I can do this. Well, it's the only thing I know."

At another point in the operation, he shouted over the loud thumping and banging of the mechanical scraper, "You have to like it, otherwise you can just forget it." He said something more but his words got shattered in the noise.

That Gene likes what he does can be seen in his easy laugh, his animated movements, his banter with customers.

Somebody has to do it. It might as well be Gene Zinani and his crew. He does them all, he says, lambs, goats, beef, hogs, deer, black widows, and bears.

(October 1980)

Cop on the Beat

I settled into the passenger seat of the police car. It was after midnight, a Thursday in early February. I had nothing else to do for the next four hours.

Harry Eiffert had been late picking me up. He'd been called to one of the taverns. He told me that everything calmed down when he walked in, that he just stood there and let the ruckus burn itself out. Another crime thwarted, and I had missed it.

Inside the patrol car the light was on. Harry wrote about the disturbance for a couple of minutes. He also jotted down the hour and minute that I joined him in the car. I was logged and recorded. Now we could roll.

We glided out of the parking lot and began the rounds. Each night-cop checks all the businesses of the town, every one of them – from the airplanes at the Twisp Airport to the elementary school, to the front and back doors of each establishment along main street. Harry himself had devised the check system.

At 2 a.m. there was a flurry of traffic as people left the taverns. The rude blatting of revved-up engines jarred the night silence of the town. "They test their mufflers to harass the pigs," Harry smiled. "I know. I've been there."

That's one thing that makes Harry such a good cop. He's been there before.

Harry appreciates the fact that being a Twisp policeman, keeping the peace in the valley, doesn't force him to wear a frown in order to appear tough. Nor does he have to be paranoid. But he's made up of finely tuned nerves and doesn't shy from admitting he gets "spooked" by any number of situations that arise.

I tried to call some of his exploits courageous but he wouldn't hear of it.

"Courage?" he puzzled. "No. I'm scared."

After a couple hours of cruising, it was clear I wouldn't get to watch Harry in action, handling deadly force, quelling some cataclysmic felony.

This was just a typical weekday February middle-of-the-night with a few dogs roaming around, mill workers making their way home at 1:30, taverns closing at 2, everyone snoring behind darkened windows. The "real thing" wasn't going to happen.

I hope Harry didn't think I was bored. Oh, no.

I got to see what he might be like if the "real thing" broke. My heart beat hard as he pulled up the patrol car fast and leapt out with flashlight at his hip to a car whose window looked jimmied. He was on that innocent car in a second. Then he backed off, came sauntering back, and got into the patrol car saying the window had obviously been that way for some time.

He had an acute eye for anything odd, askew, different, cock-eyed, crooked, bent. He knew who was parked where when, which lights weren't on before but were now, could read tell-tale tracks in the snow. Subtly he kept tabs on cars not taking the direct route to where they were supposed to be going.

When he found a pick-up truck that had worried him earlier parked in its own front yard, he relaxed and sighed, "Another crime wave solved."

Harry can laugh at himself. He must at times. Especially the time he maced himself. Trying to deliver the choking spray to a bunch of unruly dogs, Harry got on the wrong side of the wind and spent the next couple of hours sputtering and coughing. The dogs were not impressed.

We stopped on the elementary school hill for a panoramic view of town.

"This is a beautiful spot," he commented. From there he could check on chimneys, car movements, odd lights and hear different sounds. He obviously was seeing a lot more than I was. I asked Harry when the action took place.

"Actually," he said, "there's been very little crime since the force has been in effect the last two-and-a-half years." He did say that autumn is the time for domestic fights, November is suicide month, and full moon nights twelve months a year anything is apt to happen. But this was just a Thursday 3 a.m. in early February in a town with a population of 850. We kept cruising.

There weren't enough cars going by to "work the traffic", that is, to sit and point his radar at them to determine their speed. He showed me how it worked. "See, you just aim it at the oncoming cars..." A van drove by. We stared at the electronic numbers flipping silently in the dark. Eight miles over the speed limit. Surprised us both. Harry decided to check it out.

The man in the car braked fast, leapt out and came toward us. Harry was out of the car in a flash. I hunkered down in my seat. But the fellow had a legitimate excuse and Harry let him go after checking his ID. Back in the police car Harry had radio central run a check. An Oregon license plate. Panned out OK. Harry wrote it all down.

We never went farther than two or three miles from town center, yet Harry puts 50 or 60 miles per shift on his rig.

"There's a method to patrolling," he explained. "It's a way of keeping everyone honest: never do your checking in the same pattern twice."

Harry is as conscientious as they come. He'd probably be a wreck if he had to take night shift in downtown Chicago. But he takes his job no less seriously.

"When a place gets hit, I take it personal," he said. He gives juveniles breaks since "there are darn good kids around here." Knowing most of the people around has its advantages and disadvantages. But wearing the blue uniform will always attract at least some abuse no matter what. "You have to get tough-eared," he quips.

Around four in the morning, near the end of his shift, Harry parked the car on main street for the final door check.

As I bid him a fair good night Harry was striding off down the dark street shaking hands with the town's principal doorknobs for the second time.

Town felt safe. Harry was on the beat.

(February 1980)

In the Lane, Pearl Is Glistening

On Tuesday afternoons, Pearl Clark hangs out at the bowling alley. She's 83.

Eyeing the pins way down that hardwood lane, Pearl walks up to the firing line and rolls the ball the distance. Her right arm follows through above her head, and there she keeps it suspended as she watches the ball's slow progress down the alley.

If the hit is good, her big smile flashes on and she wheels to face the accolades of her fellow bowlers, senior citizens like herself.

"Good going, Pearl," one applauds.

"Just like a pro," comments another. "Just like you knew what you were doing."

If she's thrown a gutter ball, she waits patiently for it to return, then tries again.

Pearl often breaks a hundred. A newspaper clipping in her pocket persuades unbelievers she had a particularly good week last April.

Organized last year, the once-a-week gathering of senior citizens at the Methow Valley Lanes has provided good times during the slow cold months. The management offers them a game, plus shoes, for one dollar.

Bill Westlake, 70, just switched to his left hand this year after pulling a muscle in his right arm. Nevertheless, he bowls well. After knocking over most of the pins on his first roll, he turns and says with a smile, "And I can hardly stand up!"

Pearl Clark

Mertice Phillips and her husband had never bowled before joining the group. "What am I doing wrong today?" she mock-wails after her ball finds a better route, via the gutter, on its way to the target.

"You're not hitting the pins!" laughs Les Dorris, knowing he can get away with a jibe. Aware of each other's aches and pains, they laugh and joke and encourage one another. Winter Tuesdays pass a little faster that way.

(December 1986)

Back-to-the-Lander

Put a hippy and a businessman in the same room, they'd give each other wide berth. A workaholic and a kayaker don't often cross paths. A serious person and an easy joker are sometimes at odds.

But blend all the qualities of these disparate characters and you come up with Barry Stromberger, a Winthrop auto mechanic who lives in a teepee, a man who lives simple and thinks complicated.

"The teepee is my ashram," he says, "my one saving place where I get away from technology."

His canvas home swoops conically over a wood floor. In the center stands one of his own welded barrel stoves with a glass window for watching the burning logs. A low bed with four newly carved posts stands nearby. That is all. The teepee perches on a hill, and the Sawtooth Range and Gardner Mountain and Goat Peak ring his horizon.

Twenty paces away is his cook shed, a compact cabin with wood stove, shelves lined with home-canned vegetables and fruit, one commodious chair, a wooden counter, hanging plants slightly nipped by the recent freeze, a full bookshelf.

"I look around at this place and can tell what state my mind is in," he says. "If the wood is split and neatly stacked, if everything is in order, then my life is together, I've got it under control. If it's in a mess, then my life is fragmented; I've got too much to do and I'm not getting it done."

He claims the state of the cabin at present indicates his life is in disarray. I look around and find it tidy. Obviously his inner senses are more finely tuned than mine.

Fifty yards away is his work shed, the Slag Works, he calls it, where he does his metal work, his welding of farm tools and stoves, and his creative work.

His hours are odd. He usually works on engines the entire night, from 7 p.m. until dawn.

He likes it that way. The town closes down, he's alone after the bars shut, the whole town is silent. His. One night he looked up from his convoluted world of combustion engines and saw snow falling heavily. He put down his wrench, strode out into the intersection of main roads and sat down cross-legged, and "made peace with the snow and the night and the town."

Raised in Pasadena, he graduated from California Polytechnic in industrial technology where he was "programmed" for middle management. Suddenly he confronted the "What now?" dilemma.

A certified conscientious objector to the Vietnam War, he became a book mender and driver of bookmobiles.

In September 1973 he and a girlfriend traveled footloose into the Methow Valley to visit a friend. The visit turned into the duration. He spent the next couple of years "seeing if he could live in this radical environment."

For a suburbanite, this north country was indeed radical. For the first time he encountered chain saws, adzes and froes and became intimate with silence, fire-building, starlight, making do with less, and snow.

He began to know what it felt like to receive a whole community's approval or disapproval for what he was, or wasn't.

"The first couple of years here I lived up the Rendezvous and was considered a hippy," he says. "It wasn't until I started working in town that people began calling me by my name."

Talking about work, he says, "I've got nothing against it as long as it doesn't rule my life. There's more to life than working my butt off. I can't be all that self-righteous about it since I have no family to take care of. There's only me, now. But I've geared my life down and I want to keep it cranked down, so I don't have to make a whole lot of money. Oh, some people think work rules my life, but I look around at others in this valley and I begin to think I'm a lazy person."

Barry feels that a subtle and sometimes not-so-subtle pressure exists in the valley, a pressure to work. If you don't work, you have no validity, is how he sees it.

"I've watched people come into the valley," he continues, "and they come with a dream: to build a log cabin on ten acres, have some peace. They find they have to ski three miles into their place in the winter and sooner or later the economics of their situation hits them and they have to change their trip.

"My work feeds me, not only economically, but egotistically and creatively as well. I like to do it well and I do it as well as I can. I don't want to leave the valley to make money. Temporarily pulling up my stakes would be impractical.

"Besides, I've never experienced boredom here. Boredom is a complete unknown. Last year when I had hepatitis, I was sick for three months. I lay in my sleeping bag in the loft of the cook shed and did a lot of reflecting. Being self-employed I had nothing to fall back on. They wanted to give me food stamps, but I had food, I didn't need stamps."

On the whole Barry gets along well with the other Winthrop businessmen, despite their resentment of his opposition to development. He is perfectly aware of the valley's economic problems, and knows that something has to be done to make the valley more stable. At the same time he is wary about what must be traded to make it so.

"It's hard being a newcomer and feeling you have to say that this or that in the area is wrong. But I feel strongly the responsibility of not ruining another beautiful place. I want to live here all my life. If things go crazy, I'll have to work my butt off just to pay my taxes on these five acres."

The pure lines of the teepee say a lot about what Barry wants and is. But periodically his balance is upset by a shattering fact: the approach pattern for planes landing at the smokejumper base goes right over the teepee.

Going back to the land is hardly ever as easy as it sounds.

(February 1979)

Cowhorse/Cowboy

Eldene Johnson

One morning last week, Eldene Johnson–spurred, chapped, and gloved–swung himself onto the back of one of the finest cutting horses in the country.

Fritzy was ready to go. Show horse or not, this stallion wanted to get moving into the cold, early morning pastures of the Thurlow ranch. He wanted to show he could perform on the job just as well as he had in the arena this summer.

Those familiar with Quarter Horse cutting horses will understand that Fritzy's bloodlines are impressive. He is a Doc Bar-Tivio-King Fritz cross, generated from the felicitous conjugation of Doc's Dee Bar and Hi Fashion Chex.

Eldene first saw the horse this summer in Lynden, Wash., during Fritzy's second excellent showing in a Snaffle Bit Futurity. In his debut in Hermiston, Ore., he placed first during the preliminaries, an impressive start for a three-year-old horse. Eldene has continued Fritzy's training since August.

Last week on the Thurlow ranch it was time for branding, castrating, ear tagging and notching, dehorning and vaccinating. For the first time in Fritzy's life he would be tested as a real worker. This was to be no practice session with "play" situations.

The handsome Quarter Horse , already growing a thick chestnut winter coat, isn't large but it accepted Eldene – who is not a small man – with ease. Together they moved across the still-frosted fields, Fritzy's steamy breath punctuating the cold sunny air.

Eighty-two-year-old Frank Thurlow, who has raised cattle on this land since he was a boy, offered me a cushy seat beside him in his '79 Ford Fairmont. We drove up into the extensive homestead pastureland and winter-stopped alfalfa fields. Diane Thurlow, Fritzy's owner, rode Cowboy. Fritzy, Cowboy and the Ford Fairmont coaxed a good-sized herd of heifers, calves and steers from the high fields. The herd found itself in a complex system of corrals and branding chutes.

With the cattle corralled, Fritzy became the star of the show. His footwork on the frosty ground was an intricate ballet. Eyeball-to-eyeball with the madly rushing cows Fritzy was calmly in control. He sweated freely in the supreme effort of his dance. He split heifers from their calves on Eldene's cues, made through minute changes in rein or body position.

Fritzy moved with utter calm into another corral of almost fence-to-fence cattle, not spooking the wary beasts and waiting for Eldene's slightest command. Responding instantly and instinctively, this well-bred and well-behaved stallion began even finer work than before in a smaller, more crowded area.

Later, everyone broke for a sumptuous noonday meal topped off with apple pie and steaming coffee, served to all hands by Lucille Thurlow, who has cooked for ranch crews for six decades.

Meanwhile, Fritzy dried off while he munched hay by himself.

"Finest cutting horse I've ever ridden," Eldene commented quietly. And he's ridden plenty.

(November 1980)

Bread Truck Driver and Poet

Up at 3:45 a.m. every weekday, Ken Addis admits that he shaves, showers and dresses with his eyes closed. "I wake up halfway here," he jokes.

The Holsum Bread truck driver lives in Chelan just a few minutes away from the warehouse where he loads the bread that's arrived from Spokane in the middle of the night. After delivering to Pateros and Brewster, he heads upriver to Twisp and Winthrop.

"I don't feel like an outsider," he said. "I feel more like a resident of the Methow Valley. In fact, I have a lot more personal friends here than I do in Chelan. This is a fantastic valley: it has more friendly people per square inch than anywhere else, no kidding."

Ken has been bringing the valley its bread for 25 years, five days a week, logging a million and a quarter accident-free miles in the process.

"People ask me if I ever get bored with all that driving," he went on. "Never. This valley is so pretty and every day it changes, if you just look and SEE. I've never gotten tired of it in twenty-five years."

Not one to barrel blindly up and down the road, Ken stops his truck to watch an eagle wheeling in the sky, to take a swim in the river, or to eat his sack lunch under a tree while looking up at the hills.

Our bread man may be something of a poet. Says he, "If you want to do something fantastic, just go up into the mountains on a fall day and lie under a tamarack tree. When the sun comes through the needles you feel you're engulfed in an ocean of gold."

(May 1979)

Twisp's Barber Gripes

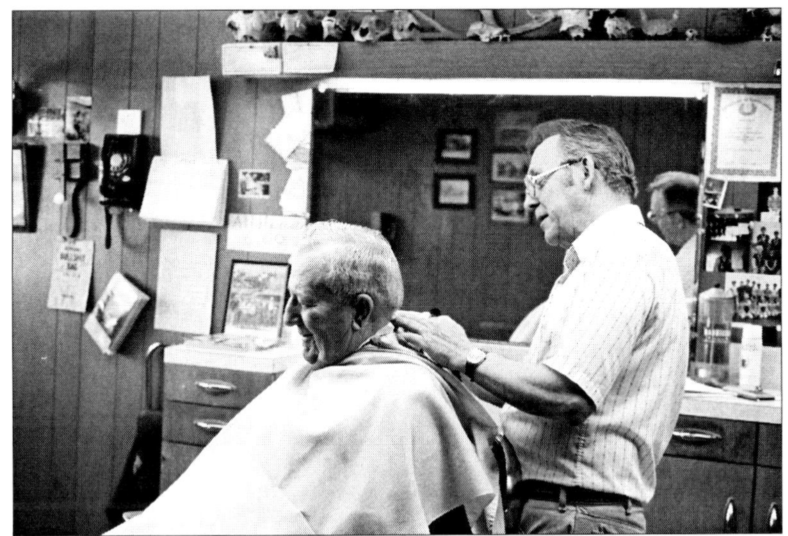

Dan Johnson clipping Howard Weller

He doesn't mind rolling double-or-nothing for a haircut.

In fact, it happens fairly frequently, says Dan Johnson, sole proprietor of the Methow Valley's only barbershop, a fixture on Twisp's main street.

If a customer wants to shake for the cut, Dan gladly sweeps the red dice from the counter where he keeps his shears and combs, flings them into the corner of the shop and watches as they bounce across the linoleum.

The customer takes his turn, and if he wins, he walks out groomed and grinning.

If he loses, he'll fork over 12 bucks. Dan will usher him to the door. "Glad to do business with you," he'll remark, patting his pocket.

While this scene shows a certain easy camaraderie with the public he serves, Dan is quick to point out that things have changed since he moved to the Methow Valley 15 years ago.

In the Western-motif town of Winthrop where he opened his first barbershop in the valley, Dan grew a handlebar moustache, wore a garter on his sleeve, and generally played the role of friendly maitre d' in a clubhouse where local cronies could gather to deal endless games of pinochle or gab away the afternoons.

Not so, anymore.

Today, on the table by the window, the cribbage board and a couple of decks of cards sit idle for weeks on end. The reason isn't all that easy to figure out. Of course, several of those charter members of Dan's emporium have graduated to the Eternal Clubhouse in the sky.

But aside from that, Dan blames himself.

"I'm grimmer," he admits. "I used to be a good mixer, good in so-called public relations. I kept a lot of my opinions to myself and kept the atmosphere light. Now, I say what I feel. I'm openly for and against things. Even if I don't expound on politics, people in this small community know what mine are. I mean, I could call myself 'Daniel, the stylist,' but I'd still be Dan the redneck barber."

He thinks people take life more seriously. The mill has closed down, ranchers are in debt, the promised ski hill has not materialized. In the last 15 years controversy has fragmented a valley that once was innocent.

As Dan sweeps up a few hours' accumulation of snippings, it is clear the pile isn't large and the color is amazingly grey.

"The size of this pile isn't really an indication of how many customers I've had today," he points out, "but how much hair they had to come off. Some of them have very little left.

"Frankly, if it wasn't for grey hair, I'd be up a creek," he notes.

Dan does not lure the teenage crowd. "It's the fashion for young people to go to beauty parlors," he explains. "It's not that I've given them a rotten haircut in the past."

Dan may feel grimmer, but when the barber pole revolves slowly outside his shop, it's nice to know he's in. He still gives a good cut, still shoots the breeze, still rolls double-or-nothing. If he feels he's gotten too opinionated for his own good, he should realize that strong opinions get the blood circulating, and good circulation makes for healthier (and faster growing) hair.

(April 1987)

Methow's Mobile Landmark

Riddle: what's smoother than the side of a refrigerator, sports a long beard blacker than coal in snow, and travels like a streak of sunlight?

Answer: the Methow Valley's mobile landmark, serious runner Willard Brooks, garbed in his florescent yellow Odlo "slime suit."

For the past eight years, Brooks' striking bald and bearded countenance has snagged the eyes of motorists along the valley's highways. But more recently, ever since he expanded his running wardrobe by two new body suits, one an eye-searing gold, the other a chrome-glittering silver, people have been pulling over just to watch him pass.

"The other day, someone rolled down his window and told me I was melting the snow," Brooks laughed.

Loping through the brown and white late-winter landscape, Brooks in either get-up is easily one of this dreary season's happiest sights.

"They certainly see me," he acknowledged.

Brooks, who turns 50 next year, logs 100 miles a week, and is most frequently seen running from his house in Twisp to Winthrop and back – a 20-mile jaunt.

Running became a passion for Brooks at the age of 41, shortly after kicking a three-pack-a-day cigarette habit. He gained 20 pounds after quitting smoking, and so responded to an invitation to participate in a local relay.

Since then, he has run two marathons a year in Seattle and continues to better his time. So far, he has placed in the top third in his age group.

Brooks moved to the Methow Valley in 1944 at the age of seven. After high school he taught ballroom dancing at an Arthur Murray studio in Seattle, worked for Boeing, and bartended. He returned in 1968.

When he isn't keeping books at Sun Mountain Lodge, Brooks streaks down the highways or through the hills, keeping in shape for marathons, and getting "runner's high."

"It's free and legal," he grinned.

(March 1987)

Model Hippy Turns Born-Again Capitalist

"I've found it!" she declared, laughing and throwing her arms in the air. "I've found capitalism!"

Ela Bannick, wife of Cloud and mother of Omaste, Sage, Sy and Shena, today is a self-proclaimed, born-again capitalist.

She and Cloud run the successful Bear Creek Lumber Company in the Methow Valley and are partners with other Winthrop business people dedicated to several enterprises.

If you'd spied Ela a few years ago you might never have guessed she would soon be admitting, as she did the other day, that she "lives, sleeps, drinks business," continuously devises ways to make money grow, and loves it.

For several years Ela lived the life of a model hippy. Her mother, Betty Wason, wrote a book about her, "Ellen: A Mother's Story of her Runaway Daughter," that appeared in Reader's Digest Press in 1976. It detailed Ela's exhausting existence for the six years she wafted around the globe, wearing "cast-off and disreputable clothing as a banner of rebellion against materialism," doing "whatever the impulse of the moment suggested."

Ela grew up in Westchester County, New York City's affluent bedroom community, surrounded by culture and steeped in the pressure to succeed in accepted ways. Instead of falling into line, Ela began disassociating herself from that scene.

"For a couple of years I put about 30,000 to 35,000 miles under my belt," Ela recalled with a trace of wonder. "I had a compulsive desire to see the world. I wanted to taste everything. I was very greedy." She seldom stayed in one place for more than two weeks.

"It's like watching a dream walker," Betty Wason wrote in her book. Perplexed and depressed, she followed her daughter's erratic meanderings, never knowing where Ela's next letter would come from.

In Morocco Ela met Cloud, another comrade disenchanted with materialism. After traveling together for some time, they started aiming for a more settled existence. They returned to the United States and lived in urban and rural communes around the country.

From compulsive traveler Ela turned compulsive survivalist, throwing herself into learning all she could about growing her own food, tanning leather, sewing all their clothes, recycling, Indian ways, "waiting for industry to burn itself out, waiting for the civilized world to die."

Ela Bannick

In 1976 four Bannicks arrived in the Methow Valley because Cloud had landed a Forest Service job. They discovered the Methow had the family-oriented community they'd sought.

For two years they lived in a teepee. Living on practically no money, they traded work for five acres, over which their home and business now sprawls.

Cloud traded labor for logs with which to build their home, and with their last pennies he bought a truckload of cedar lumber. Selling the surplus, he bought another load of lumber with the profits. Bear Creek Lumber Company was born. Today, the Bannicks employ nine people, Ela has a secretary, and they sell lumber from Florida to Alaska.

"What we're doing now is a 180-degree change from where we were," she admitted. "But we bring into the business memories of who we were. Sure, we're out to make a profit, but not at the expense of our souls. We have conscience. For us, capitalism does work. We both feel rewarded. Cloud and I have supported each other through all our changes."

As she's done in the past, Ela has thrown herself wholeheartedly into the life at hand: she is enthusiastically plugged into the '80s. Besides, she knows there's no contradiction in change.

(November1986)

Hungry Man in the Methow

Jim Evans

Sitting on the doorstep in the sunshine honing his hunting knife, Jim Evans looks just like the kids' granddad. Well, he is now, really. He'll do just fine as a granddad even though he never had any children of his own and the kids don't have any real granddads left.

Wolf Creek Road slumbers this June Sunday. The kids and their mother Irene watch Lassie on TV, and their dad George springtooths his field out past the doorstep where Jim hears the river sliding by. There's not much meat on Jim. He looks like a sparse meal for a hungry bear, but his eyes dance. We compare our knives.

Most of his life Jim has been a hungry man. Times were when a fistful of dandelions looked to him like filet mignon. He once carried salt and hot peppers in his pocket so he could jerk a skinny jackrabbit if no one else was chasing it, or add some tang to carrots found tossed out behind a grocery store.

So how did he get to heaven (Wolf Creek) from the Bruce Hotel? He says it all began when he had a stroke back in 1975. Most good things don't start with a stroke, but this one did. Who knows what brought on the illness. Jim was nearing the evening side of 60 and sleeping in orchards under newspapers, so perhaps that may have put a strain on his system.

They slapped him in a hospital bed in a room with Reuben Remsberg, George's dad. All sorts of Remsbergs visited Reuben, and since Jim Evans was right there and a friendly sort of guy, they visited him, too.

The Remsberg family kept in touch with Jim. For years they kept track of him until finally George told Jim he'd be more than welcome on Wolf Creek, preferably to stay, if he cared to.

"They just adopted me," Jim said. "They kept saying come on up here, spend some time. Well, OK, I'll visit a weekend, I said to myself. Opening day of fishing season. I went right back to Chelan and packed my bags."

Simple as that.

Irene and Jim exchanged some teasing banter.

"He'd think I was sick if I didn't give him a bad time," she smiled. Jim took a long drag on his Vantage and nodded, comfortable.

"This is the one vice I got left," he explained. He quit drinking point-blank after leaving the hospital. He said he just lay in the Cashmere rest home thinking and figuring, and realized he wouldn't be able to pay rent and keep drinking, too.

"I drank since I was about so high," he said, holding his palm two feet above the rug. "And smoked since I was his age," indicating Shawn, six.

He was most hungry as a kid, at least until he started building bridges. Fifty cents an hour allowed him to "eat up a storm" of 40-cent steaks, 30-cent ham and eggs, a dozen oysters for two bits.

When flush, he had a trick: buy a 15-cent can of corned beef and a loaf of French bread, split the bread, slice the meat into it, add salt and pepper and eat a little at a time. Last him three days. He'd wrap it back up carefully each time.

"I always stocked up," he stated.

During the Depression he was on the bum, living in hobo jungles along railroad tracks among hundreds of other hungry people. When he could, he'd help himself to a garden, just a handful, or gather pigweed, berries, wild watercress, or fruit, "ripe or green, it didn't matter."

It was then he got to like the Northwest. And that's how he found himself working in Wenatchee orchards and ending up in the hospital with a slight stroke, and meeting Reuben and the Remsbergs.

"These people here are wonderful," he confided after Irene left the room. "The whole family is. I'm happy with a warm place to live and something to eat."

And that's how Jim Evans got to be on Wolf Creek in the sunshine honing his knife.

(July 1980)

Newcomers

Janet and Bill Lindsay

Old-timers have lots to say about the Methow Valley because they've been here so long. Same for newcomers here just a short time. Enthusiasm creates a million words.

Don't think moving here these days is any easier than it was 80 years ago. The same question on the mind of those driving their cattle up the valley in 1900 echoes in the mind of today's migrants: "Are we going to make it here or not?"

But only the question is similar. While most newcomers don't rely on fickle nature to provide for their animals and land, success here is hardly a foregone conclusion. Look at the record. We don't have much population, but it's grown to include the retired Ph.D., the novelist, the scientist, the artist, the test pilot, the corporate executive. Many of these people had high-paying, high-powered jobs elsewhere and decided to chuck them.

Bill and Janet Lindsay are a fair example of those discovering Methow charm and moving here with fingers crossed. Each one left an important job to build a different dream.

Janet, a biochemist, studied DNA Polymerase in a complex of guarded buildings at Oakridge National Laboratory in Tennessee. For the past three years in San Francisco she inquired into the "brains" of cells.

Though at her career peak last year she didn't feel good about her work. "When you work with recombinant DNA there are inherent hazards," she said. "You have to use trace amounts of certain viruses and radioactivity to tag the cells and I realized that radioactivity was cumulative."

It soon became clear that she should stop toying with the idea of moving to a healthier climate. She should act, or forget it.

Bill, also a research biochemist, recently had finished an innovative project for the California Academy of Science on the Coelacanth, a prehistoric fish once presumed to be the biological link between fish and land animals. He proved it to be different.

He, too, left this heady research to move to a place where he had no name.

They were both offered jobs in Eugene, Oregon, but "Eugene just didn't have the appeal of the Methow. Eugene was practical. This is more like a dream."

After 10 months on Wolf Creek, mostly spent building their home, Janet still doesn't regret their decision.

"I'm still glad," she said. "But I'm scared. It's scary to leave what you've done for so long. Now we have to figure out how to make it here."

(February 1981)

Mobile Slaughterer

Jamie Tackman's business card certainly raises eyebrows. Thumbtacked to a bulletin board on Twisp's main street, it catches the eye.

Among other cards touting tax consultation, investment management or marketing research, Tackman's work has a little more flesh and blood to it.

Jamie Tackman

"Mobile slaughterer."

As sole worker for Alder Creek Farm Slaughter he goes where the killing's to be done, and does it on the spot.

Cattle, pigs, sheep and goats fall under his gun on their own home ground, saving farmers the trouble of loading and trucking their animals to a slaughterhouse.

Tackman, whose business is less than half a year old, has a corner on the mobile slaughtering market in the Methow Valley. He has all the work he wants. "It's not gangbusters," he smiles, "but then again I don't need a lot of money. It's more important for me to be content than to be rich."

Which is a good thing: Tackman only charges $16 an animal.

It takes Tackman about an hour from gunshot to final hooking of the quarters onto his truck's rail.

Today Tackman reported he'd been through "classic butchering: whatever could go wrong, did go wrong." He described a morning of pursuing escaped cows and getting stuck in thawing corral mud. But Tackman is known for his good nature, so the problems didn't faze him. He accepted a cup of hot coffee from the ranch manager's wife, and rested, leaning up against the hay wagon in the sunny cold morning. He had one more cow to turn into locker beef.

Having drained the dregs, he hoisted the animal to be gutted.

Deftly slicing the hide away from the cow's body, he said, "Butchering is like a lot of things. It's just plain old hard work."

That's pretty straightforward.

(December 1986)

Nothing's Free but Bad Advice

Eric Reiber

He strikes you as someone rooted in the soil. Solid. At home. Not menacing or menaced. Content among the tack and gear of farm life.

Eric Reiber, Methow bred for 15 of his 15.5 years, a sophomore at Liberty Bell High School, eventually wants a farm of his own.

"But nothing's free," he advises, "except bad advice." He's already as philosophical and fatalistic as any farmer.

Eric's virtually one already. He owns, maintains, and overhauls five tractors and sundry other farm machinery such as ancient binders and combines.

"I'm tractor poor," Eric conceded as he gave a tour of his unwieldy collection, but the statement seemed to give him more pleasure than pain. An Allis-Chalmers is his working tractor, the plower of snow and earth, cleaner of barnyards. An old threshing machine looms in the side yard like a dream out of the horse-drawn past. Harold Rakestraw's 1949 Allis-Chalmers contraption is a highly individualized conglomeration of parts Eric calls the Harold Special.

"He must have had a lot of confidence in himself to make the changes he did," Eric said. Eric has poured over the Special, to let the Rakestraw mechanical genius rub off on him.

Eric recently traded a 1948 or '50 McCormick-Deering ("one of those modern ones") for a Cletrac crawler. The Cletrac's clutch is in pieces but Eric has no doubt he'll have it running again soon. The binder, which looks to be in total disrepair, "is in better shape than it looks," he says.

Parked in rows in the shed loft are "millions" of his Tonka toys, the old, well-made miniature vehicles of his childhood. He's been enthralled with the apparatus of farming for as long as he can remember.

At his parents' home, he has his own workshop/garage. Everything in the place is his and paid for, he says, turning his head slowly and taking it all in. The compressor. Forge. Antique rototiller. The 1922 Fordson with steel wheels. "Ever see a spark plug like this?" he asks with ill-concealed wonder, unscrewing the plug and holding it up.

Periodically Eric gets apprehended by sharp-eyed cops who catch him pulling or driving clanking equipment through Winthrop late at night. He sneaks them back home, happy to have yet another piece to add to his considerable collection.

Eric has found his domain. He's got direction. And for now, he's home free.

(September 1985)

Weddings on the Deck

Dave Ebenger

Unlike big city lawyers, Winthrop attorney Dave Ebenger presides over a sun-filled office in the direct path of the Methow River, which dances below its several windows.

He can seldom guess what complaint a client will lay before him. And, as in many small town jobs, he plays a number of roles.

As Justice of the Peace, he marries couples in such unlikely places as "somewhere out-of-bounds on the Loup-Loup ski hill," with wedding party and judge all on skis.

As Twisp's Municipal Court judge, he listens to speeding offenders explain why the town's mph didn't quite coincide with their rpm's.

As Winthrop's attorney, he's privy to the nitty-gritty behind the most inflammatory of valley rumors.

By personal preference, Ebenger seldom touches divorces because "everyone's unhappy." He may take one if both parties are amicable, but only then.

Abhorring unpleasantness yet practicing law may strike some as baffling, but Ebenger derives great enjoyment out of a few aspects of the profession, especially Justice of the Peace.

"I've worked up a nice, respectful, non-religious ceremony," he said.

"I figure, hey, this is a big deal. I try to slow people down, and get them to feel what's about to happen. I want them to really get into their own wedding. After all, this might be the last bit of romance in their married lives."

A few weeks ago, a Virginia couple touring the country came to the Methow Valley and was smitten by the place. They decided to get married right then and there. Ebenger performed the ceremony on a deck on the lower part of the attorney's building, beside the river.

"I do a lot of weddings on that deck," Ebenger said. "It's a handy, pretty place. But I also go to houses of friends, or to Sun Mountain Lodge, or up in the hills. Anywhere in the county."

Twice a month Ebenger symbolically dons judge's robes to preside over the non-criminal violations of Twisp's citizens. He often finds he knows the accused, an occupational hazard in small communities.

"I try to be fair," he said. "I try to take everyone's position into account. I feel it's very important for our system that the people know they're getting a fair shake out of it. Usually, this is a person's only contact with the court system. A positive impression has to be made."

Born, raised and educated in cities, Ebenger decided they held no more fascination for him.

"I liked what I saw here," he said of the Methow.

(May 1987)

On the Lookout

At that elevation the silence is so complete even a fly's buzz can startle. But this summer, out of the blue above Lookout Mountain, the clear cadence of cathedral bells penetrates that quiet: the lookout on Lookout plays her dulcimer.

Isabelle Spohn, who just finished her sixth season as lookout for the U.S Forest Service's Twisp district, is aware of the poetic innuendos of her job, the assumed romance of spending a summer alone on a mountain top.

Keeping an eye out for smoke is not exactly drudgery. But when Isabelle first began as firefinder, she was rigidly conscientious. Every 15 minutes she took a 360 degree visual reading, section by section, which took her 10 minutes. Now, with six years of practice, she is so familiar with the terrain and so adept at seeing, she can detect the least suspicious smoke at a glance.

The room of windows balancing atop three flights of steps commands a 360-view of the Twisp River Valley, the Methow Valley from the Chewuch to Gold Creek, and over the Loup Loup into the Okanogan. The tower's centerpiece is the Osborne Firefinder, a circular precision instrument with moveable eyepiece and wire, strung diagonally over a map of the countryside. When the lookout spots "smokes," the Osborne, read correctly, can pinpoint the fire. The spotter then radios the specific location to Okanogan headquarters.

"It's addicting," Isabelle says. She scans the four horizons, penetrating the crannies of the ranges swooping into the distance. Public radio provides the scene's appropriate musical accompaniment. At least when Isabelle's not playing her own music.

At 9 a.m. Isabelle radios her presence to her dispatcher, who, in the numbery lingo of the Forest Service, acknowledges her message.

This summer, Isabelle works five days nine-to-six on Lookout Mountain. Every evening she walks out and drives home to Carlton. Every morning she hikes the long mile in (and up) by nine. Periodically she chooses to stay overnight.

For three years she tended the lookout post on North Twentymile, the most remote tower still extant on the Twisp and Winthrop districts. It perches on a ridge seven miles by trail from the road. She preferred the schedule then, 10 days on, four off.

Isabelle, who at first feels intruded upon by visitors, never fears loneliness.

"It can be really creative," Isabelle explains. In solitude she can exploit her many talents: photography, writing, reading, crocheting, observing wildlife, music (she built the dulcimer herself and taught herself to play).

She is seldom frightened. However, once a tap-tap-tapping on the window in the middle of the night at North Twentymile woke her. It wasn't a strange mountain prowler but a great horned owl wondering what the devil windows were all about.

Isabelle has been treated to some rare sights while holed up in her glass towers. Once at North Twentymile, day turned night black, the outside world disappeared, and Isabelle could hear other lookouts reporting lightning strikes. Her tower stood in the fury's direct path. As its cabin began shaking and shutters flapping, she hopped on an insulated stool to avoid becoming a lightning rod. She perched there for two hours.

A faint blue glow along the edge of a shutter caught her wide-eyed attention. The flagpole glowed, too. Seven shutters were soon etched in eerie miasma, and as the rain fell full force she watched as St. Elmo's fire formed curtains of liquid blue, and all for Isabelle's benefit.

In 1953, manned lookouts numbered 5,060 across the country. In the 1960s, aerial surveillance and changing economics reduced the number of towers to a token few. However, backcountry expert Ira Spring surmises lookouts will remain. He notes that lookouts consistently spot more fires than do aircraft; they act as weather stations, record the path of lightning strikes, and provide human contact with forest users.

He says that technology might become so expensive that it will be cheaper to hire people for the fire season.

Plus, on the human side, one has to consider romantics like Isabelle. What more perfect outlet could there be than a lookout?

(October 1983)

Young Old-Timer

Garry Dufresne

Garry Dufresne, 31, talked recently about what it meant to grow up in the Methow Valley and what he sees happening in the wake of the 1972 opening of the North Cross State Highway.

Born in 1953, Garry grew up in Mazama and Winthrop, went all 12 years of school in the valley, left for several years to seek "the real world," and then returned. Never one of the gang, Garry nevertheless feels the valley is a distinct and powerful part of himself and acknowledges that his family and this valley not only tolerated but nurtured his independent thinking.

"You're a thinker, Dufresne," a family friend once told him, "and thinkers don't have it easy." He was once beaten up at school because he refused to play football. "I just wasn't interested in what I thought football was about, " he said.

Garry admits he has mixed feelings about the Methow. The undeniable beauty of the environment and the unquestioned warmth and security he felt from his family were "priceless" but, he continued, "it was a place of small minds."

There was a staleness, he elaborated, a sameness in the life.

Psychedelics, introduced into the valley about the time Garry was in high school, had a profound effect on him. When "back-to-the-landers" began trickling into the Methow around 1970, Garry was glad to see them. While many considered the new people suspect, Garry welcomed the new blood, the new ideas. He felt they didn't have the same limitations as people he'd known all his life.

After high school Garry hit the road. The Methow native with the mystical bent studied Eastern philosophies, body massage, yoga; he lived, studied, and worked in Los Angeles and Stockholm.

During his years away he would periodically return to the valley to touch home base. Here he bucked bales and dug ditch on local ranches.

"Those times were really positive for me," he judged. "That kind of work became a standard for my life. It was honest labor, work with integrity."

From his wanderings outside the valley, he learned limitation wasn't just a Methow trait. It was a human trait.

For the last two years Garry has been a yoga instructor locally, and has a small, consistent clientele who go to him for healing massage. Two days a week he practices his body work in Wenatchee.

Garry confesses he doesn't "know" his old schoolmates anymore; that his connections are more with the people who have moved to the Methow in the last dozen years.

This new citizenry is exerting its influence on the old way of life, Garry contends. "The long-established communities are on the verge of collapse," Garry feels. "The entity that was Winthrop is just about dead. Old-timers don't recognize anyone anymore and they can't find parking spaces. The focus has shifted from one of building a life and sustaining it to exploiting and seizing opportunities.

"I grieve for the destruction of the pristine quality of the valley. Although I tend to side with those who want to go slow and preserve that quality, I also feel a pro-ski-hiller is not necessarily more greedy than someone staking out his land and telling everyone else, 'Hands off this valley.'

"A real source of community inspiration for me has always been the women who hold bake sales, rummage sales and accomplish things like raising the Barn. The women hold the town together. But even that force is breaking down."

(February 1985)

Chapter II

Coming to Grips

I can't help thinking that valley pioneers will, in the long run, be considered far luckier than those who will have cut their teeth during the technological era. Having to come to grips with every situation in a personal and immediate way bestowed an intensity to their days and gave them the chance to prove their abilities. Their real glory may be that they had a story to tell, a good story.

In the early '20s a man named Virgil Vance took first place in the Okanogan rodeo. Announcer Bill Robler asked him if he cared to take a ride in an airplane to celebrate. He said, "Sure!," slung his saddle over his shoulder and strode on down to the field where the plane was waiting. Virgil threw the saddle over the tail section of the airplane and mounted up. The plane took off. Bill was a little worried, thinking the pilot should have tied Virgil down somehow. But he hadn't. When the plane landed, a shaken Virgil slid off. "That's the most damn leather I've ever pulled in my life," was all he could say.

As Vic and Floyd Boesel said about their presence in the Methow Valley, "We're not imports, we're the real McCoy."

The stories that follow are from real McCoys.

Ole Scott, Packer

Ole Scott

If nothing else in this story rings true, this does: They don't make them like Ole Scott anymore.

To be with him in the mountains is to be with him in his natural element. To see him riding tall on a half-broke saddle horse leading a string of pack mules over a steep Cascade pass is to see him at home.

He has this to say about his life:

"I used to think I'd like to have lived a hundred years ago when the West was just opening up, when it was really wild. But when I get thinking about it, I realize I've seen the best of it the way I like to live. When I first started coming into this back country, not many people had been here, only a few sheep herders. I'll tell you one thing, I'm damn glad I won't be living a hundred years from now."

Over his lifetime, Ole has ranched, been a fool rodeo bronc rider, and a mountain packer every season since 1934.

He has also been many things to many people. Tom Graves, fellow packer, expressed it this way:

"Every kid has his own hero. Well, Ole has been my hero ever since I was a boy. He knew how to fight, pack and ride the best of anyone else I knew. Riding broncs at the rodeo, they just couldn't buck him off."

His daughter, Fae Brown, went on, "He's the kindest, most sensitive man when it comes to animals and children. I think the reason kids take to him is because he's always himself. He never pretends to be anything other than who he is. I think he's a wonderful man. But of course, I'm prejudiced."

Last week the Scotts took their family, a few friends and me on an eight-day pack trip to Surprise Lake. As the men loaded the mules at the trailhead, one half-packed beast started bucking, threw its load, and jumped off into the trees. Ole just roared with laughter.

The dust settled and still there was laughter. Somebody eventually went into the woods to find the mule.

Said Fae, "When you've got an excited horse you don't need an excited person. Dad used to take us camping when we were children. He was just so patient with us and I know we were devils. The trails were bad and dangerous then, but he would just laugh–like he does now."

That night after setting up camp, Ole sat at the campfire and asked, "And what if we'd got up at four ayem and rush rush rush hurry hurry hurry? What for? I'm here now and plumb relaxed. This is living.

"Used to be when I'd get up in the morning before sunrise I'd fish fish fish fish fish. Now I like watching the kids fish and just ding around, maybe take a snort of the old barley corn."

As we broke camp next morning, Ole led the string of five pack mules. The trail dust rose and blended with the smell of leather and horses; the wildflowered meadows spread around us; and the fir trees combed us with their shadows.

Ole pulled up in a meadow of lupine.

"Those behind me wondered what I was stopping for," he said later. "But it was just such a pretty spot I just had to stop and take a look around."

He's been in these hills forever and still he sees the beauty and talks to the wild animals.

"You always learn something every trip," he added.

That night, after the dishes had been scraped and washed, everyone settled around the fire. Ole laid back on the ground, hands behind his head, his boots glowing in the firelight.

"By gum," he smiled, "this makes a guy feel like he'd like to live. You know, I love every minute of a campfire. But I must say I've probably walked a million miles around them in my day, avoiding the smoke."

The days in the hills passed with an almost impermissible serenity.

We lacked for nothing. For months Ole's wife, Letha, had prepared for this trip, making lists of food and gear. She had remembered it all, from thread and needle to chain saw, from camp bacon to darts for the kids, from a camera to hobbles, from hoof nippers to Alka-Seltzer.

On the last night by Surprise Lake, Ole took his place by the fire, leaned back and looked up past the fir branches to the startling array of stars. He said quietly, "I can't think of anywhere else I could have lived where I could have enjoyed life more."

(August 1977)

Tom Farrow, Logger

Tom Farrow

Tom Farrow, living alone with his dog up Poorman Creek, was out of matches. He patiently leaned over his electric stove and held the cigarette to the coil until it started to smolder, "Just like an old Arkansawyer, I guess," he chuckled.

He walked slowly, limping slightly back to his chair, turning the television off on the way. His faithful friend Pepper clacked his claws on the linoleum, pacing the floor. "He's old; he doesn't know what he wants," Tom explained. "I feel pretty strong about my dog. I'd be lost without him."

Tom's careful gait indicates not only his 74 years but the time he spent on the wet side of the mountains rigging trees in the early days of steam logging.

"You spend four, five hours limbing a tree one hundred, one hundred fifty feet high all the way to the top, you'd feel it," he nodded, then leaned over and described the strapped shingear fit with a four-inch steel spur that allowed him purchase on the thick-barked coastal trees, timber he turned into spars for cable rigging.

"Height didn't bother me," he claimed, "but when I started I was nervous. They used to sway quite a bit when you topped them." After the swaying stopped, he'd hoist himself up onto the very top and sit there, smoking a cigarette.

"Men didn't amount to much them days; they were a dime a dozen," he explained, talking about the big logging companies' attitude toward their work force. "It didn't bother those companies to lose men."

In 1940 he and his wife and four children moved to the Methow Valley. "To be honest with you, I don't know what I came over here for. Just liked the country, I guess."

Tom got a job falling timber up Myers Creek with Gus Smith for Claud Wilhelm, and also for John Garner. Falling was a new job for Tom.

"Tom was a good partner on the crosscut," Gus said, paying Tom the ultimate compliment.

He also worked for Wagner in the woods Cat logging. "I never did relish a Cat," he said. "They're log getters but they're slow. That steam yarder on the coast was wicked and fast and it killed a lot of men. They'd get going so fast the cables would tighten, break off and hit a snag just disintegrating it.

"Guys ask me around here what's the biggest log I ever put a choker on. I tell them nine feet, nine inches. People just shake their heads, think I'm lying. Up the Chewack I've seen them five foot through, had to use two chokers bridled, anyway."

Tom retired in 1973 from working for the Forest Service on fire lookout. "I hated it," he said about being on Leecher Mountain Lookout. "It was lonely, or the hunters pestered me. I wouldn't take that job now for a thousand dollars a day."

Tom says he wouldn't go back to the west side of the state, even though he's lonely here. His dog Pepper is his main concern, and Tom figures he'd get lost over there.

"I don't own him, he owns me," he said as he got up and lit another cigarette on the electric coil. "Eats better than I do, too," he smiled. "But he never talks back."

(July 1981)

Charley Barcelou, Moonshiner

Charley Barcelou

The way I met Charley Barcelou is the way I meet many people: I walk up to their houses and knock.

One morning I drove to Carlton, made a couple of dog-leg turns, stopped and walked past a garden of bean rows and tomatoes to the back door of an old farmhouse. The sunlight ricocheted off the white boards and the yard was full of peace. I knocked, and Grace Barcelou, Charley's wife, asked me in. Charley held onto my hand a nice long time, and I discovered I had to bellow to be heard.

"I got good eyesight," Charley, 93, mentioned, "but when someone talks, it sounds like they've got their mouth full of mush, like Donald Duck."

Once in a while you meet someone and like him right away. You feel he's solid, "good as gold," as neighbor Ross Filer called Charley. That's the way I felt.

A privilege of those in their nineties is to say what they feel, say what they did, smoothly, so it's done and felt and gone, and they can look back, smile and raise their eyebrows about their own exploits.

During Prohibition Charley made whiskey up Texas Creek, as a number of people did. But what distinguished him from other moonshiners was that he tried to do it well. Bill Robler told me that.

"Charley made GOOD moonshine; he was fussy about it," he said.

Charley told me as much. You could tell by the way he described the process of making it in big tubs over seven or eight days that he did it right, did it clean, and it was prime goods.

He told of keeping the filter clean, of filtering the corn or fruit mash through charcoal, and through several thicknesses of flannel and silk.

"Nobody gets poisoned that way," he stated. "You got to run it slow," he went on, as if the need still existed. "If you boil it fast, you boil the mash. What you want is to keep it slow so you get alcohol before the water goes up in steam."

In this valley a lot of people weren't half as conscientious as Charley about making good liquor. He recalled one still (he never mentioned names) where the tubs weren't covered and "blowflies and yellow jackets were two inches thick" all over the surface of the contents.

One time Charley dumped some of the used cracked corn into his hog's trough and the swine gobbled up the heady feed.

"That pig was drunk for two whole days," he laughed. "He was a white pig and his ears turned bright red. I drug him around 'cause all he did was sleep."

And burp happily, no doubt.

(October 1979)

Flora Belle Hix, Switchboard Operator

Flora Belle Milliman Hix, 77, lives housebound two blocks from Winthrop's main street, abiding solitude gracefully.

Once, however, Flora Belle was in the hub of things. As a telephone operator during the 1920s at Winthrop's West Side Telephone Company, she roused the doctor in emergencies, rallied townspeople during fires, recruited forest firefighters, and even broadcast the war news.

"I still dream about it," she admits.

Despite wages of 15 cents an hour (45 cents after 13 years), Flora Belle led an interesting and sometimes exciting life at the telephone exchange.

She did indeed live within earshot of the switchboard, at first with her parents and later with her husband. The switchboard closed at 8:30 p.m., but she wasn't free to go very far away. Flora Belle was the "scanner" in those early telephone days.

Often during the night the emergency buzzer would shatter her sleep and she would rise, light the kerosene lamp, and deal with the problem.

"Babies come at night generally, you know," she says. Many a time she had to reassure the caller, ring the doctor from his sleep and explain a baby wanted to be born.

When fire broke out, she was the first informed. Immediately she would ring the emergency alarm to everyone with a phone and tell them where the fire was burning. The rush was on.

Dousing a fire was a community project. If people didn't have their own bucket they'd dash to the mercantile, grab a bucket from the shelves and be off to the fire. A bucket brigade would form, everyone lining up from river or irrigation ditch to the house, passing the full and empty buckets up and down the line.

When forest fires raged in the mountains, again the operator was one of the first contacted.

"I knew everyone from Mazama to Carlton then," she says. When the call came, she'd figure out who could go into the hills for days, sometimes weeks, with a pack string to fight the blaze.

But emergency dispatching wasn't Flora's only extraordinary function. She also broadcast the news. During World War I no radios blared into valley ears, so when Flora received news about troop movement, victories and defeats in Europe, she'd phone various people about the war.

Beside the switchboard was a list of personal code rings, two shorts and a long, or whatever. Everyone heard everyone else's ring, "so everybody could rubberneck," she laughs. "And believe me, they did."

(April 1980)

Cynthia Bailey Obituary

Cynthia Lemaster Bailey, 96, was one of those extraordinary human beings whose delight in everything and everyone was as infectious as her laughter. "I just LOVE people," she declared to me one day, and that love ricocheted right back to her. Someone once said, "If you don't hear Cynthia laughing somewhere in the valley, she isn't here."

Thing is, she stayed right here for 75 years.

She detested this valley that scorching day in 1910 when she arrived by stagecoach. She prayed all night she'd survive till morning so she could get out of this snake-infested pit. After a few days she got used to it, then got to love it so much she never left until she died last Tuesday.

As Reverend Cone said at her funeral, "We're here to celebrate Cynthia's life," and the overflow crowd at Precht's Chapel cried and laughed because they'd known her.

Her immense family was there, too, spilling over into the main hall, forcing friends to sit in the anteroom and the rarely used casket room. "I really populated the area," she once laughed. At the time of her death she had 35 great-great grandchildren and one great-great-great granddaughter.

Poems written by her family and friends were read at the service, many of the verses alluding to her talents as a cook, her inability to let anyone go hungry, or let anyone gain less than five pounds at a sitting. Throughout the Depression and into the late '50s Cynthia owned and operated a string of six restaurants in the valley. Reverend Cone benefitted from Cynthia's policy of never allowing a minister to pay for his meals. She tried to retire a couple of times but her clientele had gotten hooked on her cooking, and she never could say no.

A woman sitting next to me at Precht's commented in a loud whisper to her husband, "Cynthia was one beautiful person. She was one beautiful lady." Pause. "And she was pretty, too."

Indeed she was, and her eyes never, in 96 years, lost their sparkle.

I think a good many of her friends were sitting there Friday looking forward to meeting up with her again in the Other World, where, as one of the poems rhapsodized, Cynthia'd be cooking meals for St. Peter, much to his delight.

(September 1985)

Perry Clark on Indians

The Methow River swirled around the horse's legs. Perry Clark, age 11, sat as still as he could behind the Indian. His feet were tied together under the horse's belly. Holding his breath, he and the Indian watched the undulating forms of the salmon in the refracted light beneath the river's surface. The Indian held a spear poised.

Like lightning the Indian struck. The spear danced, but he pinned the salmon under the water until it perished.

That was the way it was done. It was 1901.

"There were far more Indians than whites here during the summers at that time," Perry recalled 75 years later. One summer when Indians had come to the Methow Valley to catch and dry fish for the winter, Perry counted 32 tepees on Lake Creek.

"Us boys took a liking to those people," Perry said. "We'd go fishing with them, even though my father didn't like them too much. They took care of us, that's why they tied my feet under the horse, so I couldn't fall into the river if the horse bolted. I fished with Methow George once. He was a quiet old feller, he didn't do too much talking. And I got acquainted with Chiliwist Jim. I learned to speak their language, Chinook, and sometimes I still speak it with Bill Robler just for fun."

(December 1976)

Fae Dibble, Leaving Home

For 55 years the house sheltered, nurtured and knew only Dibbles.

Under the same roof, two people began a marriage and saw its end with the death of one. Between those walls two boys grew up, learned what life offered and left to live it on their own terms in other locations.

In this restless culture, where some Americans shed houses with the same frequency snakes shed skins, homes lived in by the same family for decades emit a rare feel of comfort and solidity, like friends who last.

But age is no mean intrusion. At 80, Fae Dibble has run out of the steam it takes to tend the gardens, and, even though she'll tell you she's no sentimentalist, the empty house must mutter about the past. Sure, like anyone who's stayed put she's accumulated a million things, and she knows her sons, like most discriminating sons, "don't want your trinkets."

Fae has left her touch on the house. Thirty years ago she chose and hung wallpaper depicting a genteel Southern scene, repeated in comforting fashion up and down the living room wall. For years the same straight-backed young man has lead the same compliant woman toward the same sedate and pillared mansion under the same never-fading oaks. To calm the eye, Fae hung quiet blue print wallpaper on the rest of the walls, and painted the rest of the house herself. She came by the work naturally.

"George was good about plumbing," she said about her husband, "and he made these shelves," she said, running her hand along the bookshelves next to her chair.

They first moved into the little house at the top of Pool Hall Hill in1930. They were freshly married. George ruled the bank; she was a science and math teacher. Honeybee Scott built them a fireplace, and another man, hard up for depression cash, dug them a basement for $10. Leonard Rader, Claud Dibble and Ed Allen built on extra rooms. Two sons were born, and Fae took a 17-year leave of absence to raise them. Then she taught for 22 more years in Twisp. For seven years Fae took devoted care of George after a stroke left him paralyzed and virtually speechless.

Fae's not moving far, and she's not moving for fear of drunks on the prowl from that wild town down the street. She's moving to the mobile home park in Twisp because many of her friends live there. Plus, she adds, "most of my friends are gone or are up at the cemetery."

The young woman who swayed into the valley in 1929 on the rocking Red Mail Coach will soon drive herself to Twisp in her snazzy maroon 1982 Chevrolet Classic. She looks forward to the move, though she'll miss the happy picnics held out under the garden trees. Otherwise, she's philosophical. Time, and Fae, march on.

(November 1985)

Ellis Peters Left Home

Ellis Peters' crowning years aren't turning out exactly the way he imagined. The other day he said, "Whenever I thought about being retired, I always pictured myself as having years and years of nothing to do but enjoy myself. But she got sick, and now I'm left all alone."

A couple of years ago he and Martha moved into the Twisp Garden Apartments, leaving their Mazama home, the one with the graceful curve to its front door eaves, the one they'd lived and loved in for half a century.

Last summer Martha died.

The overwarm apartment is quiet. Once in a while Ellis will turn on the TV to fill in the blank spaces.

"My mind's up there in Mazama most of the time," he admitted. "But it's nothing like it used to be. Now, it's full of people. But I do get a kick out of thinking of the way it was. Up there you could step out the door and see a bear, or some deer, maybe even a cougar. One morning I got up to close our bedroom window and I saw the pawprints of a cougar on the window sill."

Ellis' vision of Mazama is made up of a million events and feelings accrued over the 70 years he lived there. He still sees himself a young boy running beside the rivers and befriending Indians who camped and hunted near his folks' homestead.

Ellis often shared their food. "They had good eats," he commented. "Things like hot biscuits and potatoes and gravy. One time – I don't know if I told you this story before or not – it's sort of dirty – well, one day I saw them eating these dry, brown things about the size of a silver dollar, so I popped one in my mouth. It had a taste all its own, but something like raisins. After I'd eaten a few, a squaw laughed and pointed to a piss ant hill. They'd lured the ants into a honey jar and pressed them all together. Guess I didn't eat with them much after that," he chuckled.

Images of how the Indians caught salmon still play across his mind. One man would ride into the upriver side of a big, flat pool where he'd raise his deer horn spear and wait, stone-still. By then, a few others would have waded into the pool's lower end and begun tossing stones, scaring the fish against the current and into the lethal shadow of the man on horseback.

"I never saw him miss," Ellis said.

Possibly, there's no one else alive who remembers how the smell of camas roots, dug at Harts Pass by the Indians and stored at the Mazama post office, would linger in that building nearly all winter. "It smelled good and strong, but kind of pleasant," Ellis recalled.

"Then the time came the Indians didn't come back so much. For some reason they didn't seem to need the smoked fish and dried berries and roots anymore. They had cars," he said.

A few years ago the Aspen Skiing Corporation bought the Peters' property. He was told by the company that his home stood near the spot they'd envisioned a ski lift terminus.

From the day in 1912 he first leapt from his parents' wagon onto Mazama soil until the sad hour he reluctantly drove away in 1984, Ellis learned countless things about Indians and animals and sawmills and loneliness and himself, about necessity and the feel of wild places. His observations span the time the land turned from hunting grounds to playground, from being the end of the road to being the beginning of a cross-state highway.

Almost every day he goes to Mazama. The best way. By memory.

Looking into the emptiness between his sofa and the apartment wall, he said to himself (but I heard it), "Twisp will never be home."

(January 1987)

George Moore, Cowman

Arthritis may have taken the spring from his gait, but you'll never find him sitting when there's work to do. If you catch him leaning on his shovel, he's not frittering away anyone's tax dollars. He's just patiently waiting for the ditchwater to run the direction he wants it to.

George Moore, 65, lean and slightly bent, keeps on the move because he raises cattle. His partner is his mother, Millie Bagwell, 82.

George never looks as if the next valley over holds more promise than the one he's in. In him, there's a stillness, born, I guess, of years spent around animals and alfalfa, things that take their own sweet time growing.

I'm often in their house buying eggs or milk. When no one's home, I walk in the door, get what I want out of the refrigerator and leave money, making change from a little dish on the cupboard shelf.

I find them home more often in winter, sitting by the wood heater, well-read newspapers set aside on the oil-clothed tabletop. Millie at rest, sunk deep into the easy chair beside the stove, is a study in perfect relaxation. She's never needed therapy to learn how to do that.

In summer their work load increases dramatically. I often see them driving their brown pickup through the valley, tending to their widely distributed herd, pastured on the best grass they can find. Often the appearance of that calf-hauling vehicle resembles a cake with chocolate frosting drizzled down its sides. If that analogy is too sweet, let's just say they'd never have to lock their doors in Seattle.

Growing up on Potato Creek near Entiat, George never spent time mooning about the city's bright lights, but would often grab a blanket, a rifle and some grub and hike into the hills for a few day's communion with the land.

Between boyhood and now, George worked a number of jobs – from firing boilers in Colorado to helping dig Leavenworth's first sewer system. To his grandchildren, though, he'd recommend the ranching life.

George had plenty of good things to say about it.

You don't have to punch a time clock.

There's something new happening all the time. Animals are interesting: they're always trying to outguess you. For dumb brutes, they're pretty damn smart, said George. They don't talk back, either; that way you THINK you know who's boss.

You're not cooped up inside.

George knows the valley is changing, but his insides aren't all tied up in knots about it. If there's more traffic when he herds his cows to and from pasture, well, that's just the way it is.

The cattle market has been lousy the last few years. "Sure it has," George shrugged, "but what are you going to do about it?"

It looks as if George will never quit. "If I sat down for a winter, I'd never move again," said the rheumatoid arthritic. "If all I did was watch TV I'd be dead within a year. I'll stay with the cattle till I drop in my tracks. That's as good a way to go as any."

If a hundred thousand dollars suddenly rained down from the ceiling into his lap the only thing he'd do differently would be to take a sightseeing trip to Alaska. You don't just drop everything because of a windfall. You don't just walk out of the barnyard and let the calves fend for themselves.

Besides, he gets attached. We walked out to the barn to take a look at several newborn calves. In the sweet haysmelling barn George sauntered over to the pen, leaned on the barrier and said, "Hi, kids."

The calves looked up. "Hiya, George," they grinned.

(March 1987)

Dick Horn Goes Back Toward Azurite

Dick Horn

Last week Dick Horn forgot that he was 86.

Monday morning in the shade at Rattlesnake Campground, Dick took hold of the saddle horn and heaved himself onto a Spanish mustang and proceeded to ride 10 miles up the Methow Trail to Horse Heaven, a lush meadow area just beneath Azurite Pass.

Forty-four years ago he traveled the same route on snowshoes, headed for the Azurite Mine, where he acted as foreman of surface operations during the mine's brief heyday, 1936-39.

On one trip into the heart of the Cascades, he just about cashed it in when a cornice of snow broke off the ridge as he topped the pass. The subsequent avalanche swept him hundreds of yards down the mountainside.

His daughter, Cathy McCauley, saw that nearly fatal slope last week for the first time and suddenly the scene she had only imagined for years took on solid flesh.

On Tuesday, Dick and Matt Olason spent several fairly grueling hours in the saddle trying to trace the trail to the summit on a scratch of a path crisscrossed with animal meanderings. Too often the trail petered out in heavy brush.

The assault failed to get Dick back to the old haunt, but Dick didn't complain. He got to sleep under tall firs and put his hands on the remains of a log cabin built for dog-sled mail carrier Ed Kikendall. He strode off into 10-foot high brush to track down logs of another cabin he knew had been swept across the Methow River during a violent avalanche in '37.

Others in the party tired long before Dick.

Although the Azurite made none of its owners rich, the main asset of that short-lived adventure could be the gold mine of stories that came out of it. Dick, back near the site, certainly was fueled by memories. It wiped the age clean off his face.

(August 1981)

Deke Smith on Growing Old

"Took me a long time to learn how to be old," said Deke Smith, 89, one day down at the Saturday Farmers' Market. Deke's eyes are none too good and he wouldn't win a race with a garden slug, so when you collar him to chat he's gotta chat because he can't get away. Besides, Deke's a philosopher, Methow homegrown type, and ideas are what he's best at.

"That's right. I'm pretty good at b.s.," he understated.

After that comment about his taking a long time to learn to be old, I tracked him down at his cabin. Cats were messing around all over the place, sunshine and flies were pouring in the open door, a bucket of newly unearthed garlic and onions sat on the doorstep. Deke turned off the radio, took his sweet time about lighting a cigarette, and told me about his getting old.

"When I was in my early sixties, I realized I was slowing down. I worried and griped, but I just kept gradually going downhill. Well, hell, I thought, that's just nature taking its course: what the heck of it? Just let nature take its course.

"People get to moaning and bitching about getting old but I just tell them, you're just fading out, that's just nature's way, let it go that way. Act your age, I say.

"Things start to run down; you keep learning those lessons all the time. You got to say: Whoop, what the hell am I doing? You got to boss yourself, remember the lessons. Never mind the other fellow.

"This up here," he tapped his head, "that's what rules the whole system. Stress, worry, it all starts up here. I know how to meditate. Think of nothing. Make your mind go blank. Just shut down. Soothe down, in other words.

"Trying to keep up with this modern 'transportation,' I call it, we just weren't made for it, for that high speed. This old world's been rolling around the universe for eons, neither faster nor slower than it ever has, but we're all speeded up. That's where high blood pressure comes from."

Deke switched the subject to politics, but it made him depressed. It made him say, "Sometimes I feel good about the fact I'm on my way out."

When Deke finally goes to sit under that Great Pine Tree in the sky and chuckle at all us old foody-doodies bumbling around on our section of the earth, one thing's for sure. It'll come very naturally to him.

(October 1983)

Helen Jackson's Six Husbands

Helen Jackson and her cat Hobat

Down in the senior citizen apartments at the edge of Twisp by the Methow River, Helen Jackson lives with her cat Hobat, her crocheting, her television, and her memories.

An Austro-Hungarian who grew up speaking Serbish, she sailed to America, gliding in under the shadow of the Statue of Liberty when she was12.

She's toughed it out ever since. She's dug sugar beets, picked navy beans, housekept, waitressed. And had six husbands.

Three of them she got from the Lonely Hearts Club, and one from an ad she wrote in the papers. The bad thing was, "They were all lemons."

She made her way to the Methow Valley in 1959 because one of those Lonely Hearts Club characters who lured her here claimed he was a songwriter.

"I married that goofus and found out he wasn't NOTHING," she emphasized. He hadn't even gotten in the firewood for the approaching Mazama winter. That marriage lasted six months.

Her first husband was a Mexican. "I'm a Mexican," he told her as she served him his coffee in the restaurant where she was working. "I'm a German," she responded. "How would you like to cross over?," he proposed. She had his son after they'd gone down to Mexico. But he was a gambler and didn't return stateside with her when she did.

Her first Lonely Hearts Club husband lasted a month. "He called himself Richards, but that wasn't his real name," she explained.

Her fourth husband was named Jackson and they were together 15 years. Then something happened. "But I kept his name, even though I married a couple more times after that. I wouldn't take THEIR names!

"I never fought with my husbands," she went on. "I just told them what. My parents fought and I decided I'd never do like that."

When things got rough, as they always did, she'd pack her bags and set out, giving life its head. "I always was full of the old Harry," she said. "I'd work for six months, then go on a binge, travel ... Nothing ever fazed me. I'm not one of those timid things," she stated. "I'm easy to get along with, but provoke me...

"Don't feel sorry for me," she once told her sister. "I'm OK. I'll fight my own battles. You know," she said, stroking long-haired Hobat purring on her lap, "I never took anything serious, even to this day. I've had a lot of fun, believe me."

The woman down at Twisp Garden Apartments at the edge of town behind the crochet needles watching soap operas has lived through a lot, but not so you'd notice.

(April 1985)

Ross Filer, 'The Cattle Come First'

On the door to Ross Filer's house is this hand-written message: "To Who This May Concern: The 'Cattle Come First.' I belong to the Cattle Ever After. find me Wherever you can. Ross."

This is Ross's story, as he told it to me:

"In 1900 my parents, Ben and Ida Filer, came to this valley. They had a wagon and a buggy and my dad drove the cattle ahead of them. They just grazed them along, slowly, just grazed them along. The grass was so thick, it was all headed out like wheat. And there was water in every nook. They drove the cattle right through the streets of Wenatchee.

"That first year my dad put his cattle up Poorman Creek. All he had to do was just let them out. Oh, and you had to brand them, everything had to be branded, the cattle, the horses, everything. Because some people are honest and some aren't. Well, anyway, the thing was, cattle was the only source of income they had. And of course, you needed horses. They were just as plentiful as cars are today.

"Horses, all they did was work.

"I was born in Twisp in 1903. I was the only sheep and I was a black one. I was born on the thirteenth and that's bad.

"I can remember when Twisp had one store. It was a great big store, groceries on one side, hardware on the other. Oh, it had everything. It had a great big round stove in the middle. I always wanted a stove like that, just put a big chunk of wood in and let it burn all day long.

"And then there were two blacksmith shops. They were both going all day long, they were shoeing horses all the time. I was just a little bitty tyke but I can remember.

"You know, a little boy is like a tree. He's got to get roots, but it's also very easy to get hurt.

"And then there was a harness shop/shoe shop. They had spurs and chaps and spurs and ropes.

"I used to watch them unloading freight. T.G. Johnson had the transfer business. Those freight wagons had six or eight horses. I like to see a horse pull, just as steady as clockwork.

"I remember March in 1918. I was sitting in a bobsled. The snow was deep, oh, Lord. There was a stock sale going on in town. There was a horse there, a trained cow horse. I just wanted that horse so bad. Well, my dad started to bid on him and I thought he was going to lose it. Well, he got it and put me on it. Boy, oh, boy, I thought I was somebody. That was when I started driving.

"My father was a driver also and he taught me everything I know. A man by the name of George Grant used to come to the valley and buy up old hamburger cows, they looked like the dickens, and we'd drive them down the valley. Men were scarce then, it was during the war, so they got me to drive.

"Oh, heck, I had a big time. They told me, "Now, you watch those cows. They'll sneak off on you." They were sometimes hard to keep track of. It was four days round trip to Pateros. I got $10.50 to make the trip.

"Well, we got down to Pateros with all those cattle. There was an old bridge there. That old thing would just sway and sway when you went across. When we got them to the stockyard we loaded them up in the cattle cars.

"We put hundreds of head of cattle up on the range, sometimes as many as 300 head. Batie put up 200 head, Jim Johnson, 36, the Watsons, 45 head, Joe Bonning, 97.

"We camped up there on the range all summer. We had Canyon Creek, the middle and west forks, and we had Lime Creek, and North Creek, and War Creek, and we had the Twisp River.

"I drove for a lot of guys. And I stacked hay. Father said I was the best man on the stack. I overheard him say that. I did just what he told me to. When he was dying of cancer he gave me instructions: he told me to pay off the men. I did exactly what he told me. He died in 1938.

"I took over the place. I still had my mother. We held on to the cattle and raised hay. I did everything with horses. I never did own a tractor. I had a four-horse springtooth. Even now if you gave me a field and some horses I could do it right. But with a tractor I'd get ridges.

"We kept our cattle until 1945. By then the Forest Service made it hard on range cattle. Mother died in 1949.

"Well, that just about brings you up to date.

"Riding herd, driving those cattle, doing that was my pleasure. That was my heaven. You got hot and you got cold and you worked hard, but it was still the easiest work in the world.

"It's when you can't hold your own end up that hurts like hell."

(April 1977)

Greydon Patterson, Logger

For loggers up Eightmile that winter day in 1955, operations were proceeding as normally as possible considering they had to fall trees in 14 inches of snow.

It was Greydon Patterson's turn to build the fire for lunch and set the lunch pails around it to thaw. When he'd thrown on the last piece of wood he checked his watch and saw he had enough time to go and fall one last tree before the noon whistle blew.

"I don't regret working all my life," said Greydon 25 years later. "The only thing I wouldn't have done was felled that last tree. Everything went to hell all at once," stated the wiry man from Mazama matter-of-factly.

Greydon was woods-wise and no stranger to tricky situations in the forests, so he knew when he made the first cut on that four-and-a-half foot pine that it was partially rotten and he better make some side cuts fast. But the tree found its own insidious momentum, split vertically for 30 feet and began its erratic topple.

"It barber-chaired," said Greydon simply, "and run me uphill. I thought I could outrun it."

Bouncing once, the huge pine first caught the logger on the run and knocked him down. The second time it came back to earth it took his leg off below the knee.

Slim Worthen was the first man at the scene and he immediately lay down beside the fallen man and pulled Greydon over on top of him, to get him out of the snow and keep him warm while rescue operations went into high gear.

"I spent two years, six days and fifteen minutes at Brewster Hospital," he said with retrospective humor that's born of calamity long after the fact. "They didn't even set my other leg, which had been badly broke, until several days later to see if it was worthwhile, to see if I'd make it."

For Greydon, Mazama is home. He desires nothing bigger or better and lives on the same piece of ground his father homesteaded in 1910. When his parents and two brothers joggled into the valley 70 years ago they had a

Greydon Patterson

dollar and a half to their names. Today, the land they received free from the government is worth up to $10,000 an acre.

"I struck it lucky," Greydon smiled.

The family kept dairy cows on their quarter section (160 acres) of land, but the men worked out logging and at sawmills to keep the farm going. As Greydon says, "This isn't farming country. You always had to work out."

But it is snow country.

The year there were eight feet of snow on the level, 60 inches of it fell in one night. One day Greydon was up to his waist in snow when a friend spotted him. What the friend didn't know was that he was sitting on his big old sorrel saddle horse.

Greydon likes people and he can spot a phoney a mile away.

"It don't take me long to find 'em out," he claimed, then admitted he tends to think that "people were more people" back when things were a bit more basic.

Greydon's a fighter. As he judges, "You can't let life get you down."

(December 1981)

Jay Stokes, Rancher

Jay Stokes with grandson Blake

Blake, four months old, has the Stokes' eyes, but whether or not he will inherit the family birthright of farming Beaver Creek is debatable.

When he eventually comes of age and realizes that he could be the fifth generation to lease range on Frazier Creek and eke a farmer's living off the fertile Beaver Creek fields, the cycle may already have closed.

Farming the Methow has never been a path to riches. A grown-up Blake will have to choose between a way of life that may have gone out of style and the ample other opportunities, here or elsewhere, to make a living.

Jay Stokes, center of gravity for five generations of Stokes whose focus has been ranching the area, feels the prospect of Blake's continuing the business is not particularly good.

Jay's lifetime, on the other hand, has spanned the time from certain inevitability to a definite choice: from being raised on a struggling Methow ranch to a time when he was able to choose to ranch or not.

Jay is now in the process of easing himself out of the work and leaving the running of the place to his sons Morrie and Vic. Jay and his wife

Elsie are happy their sons have chosen, and enjoy, the work.

"Maybe it indicates that they're pleased with what they had growing up," Elsie mused.

In 1922 when Jay was four, the family moved down to the land that he and his sons now work. By 1929 his older siblings had left home and "that left me the oldest child at home and me going on 11. I had an opportunity to mature early," Jay concluded.

"Go look after our cows in Wolf Canyon," his father told his 11-year-old son.

"Wolf Canyon? Where's that?" gawked Jay. His father gave him sketchy directions with a wave toward the distant hills and sent him on his way. That was the beginning of Jay's responsibility for the stock.

Today, he and his sons still ride much the same terrain for their cattle. He considers it the hardest part of ranching, although he admitted he tended to feel slightly discouraged at a rancher's lot just last week while attending a calving by flashlight in "that miserable rain in a creekbed with the water running over my boot tops."

But back when he was young he enjoyed the life whole-heartedly. He has an eloquent, zesty way of telling stories about that world, a little wild, a lot dusty. What is most real to him about it is the sense of being on one's own in a world of finalities: you either made it or you didn't.

(October 1981)

Floyd and Vic Boesel Remember

Floyd and Vic Boesel

Put two brothers in their 60s in the same room to talk about their lives and they might agree so seldom the past would fog in.

But that wasn't true about Floyd and Vic Boesel. They allowed each other the benefit of their own quirks of memory and told their individual, but often neatly parallel, lives.

Oh, there were one or two raucous moments in the course of the morning's interview. A problem about Floyd's birthplace arose almost immediately.

"I was born in 1911 in a house on the main street in Winthrop," Floyd began, settling back into his easy chair.

"I wonder if you weren't born at Patterson Lake when the folks lived up there and Dad worked at the sawmill," countered Vic.

Floyd looked puzzled.

"At least I got the IMPRESSION I was born in Winthrop," he said.

"Maybe you were born on the road," Vic concluded, and they left it at that.

Later, when Vic was on the phone, Floyd was quietly recalling how many cows each of them had to milk before school when they lived on the Falls Creek homestead.

"Vic had to milk four..." Floyd calculated.

"I milked six!" Vic shouted clearly and dogmatically from two rooms away.

"Once, when I wasn't much bigger'n a peanut," Vic went on, "and we were riding home from school, the saddle wasn't cinched up tight and we must have shifted at the same time because all of a sudden we were both looking up under the belly of the horse, just stuck on there..."

"I don't remember that," said Floyd, unperturbed.

(November 1981)

One Year in the Life of Esther Spurgeon

Esther Spurgeon

For Esther Spurgeon and her family, 1924 spelled B-A-D.

Her father, Frank Parker, a fiercely individualistic and inventive man, had brought his wife and children to Boulder Creek, an unpopulated neck of the woods, even by Methow Valley standards. He felt he needed to get away so he could vent his creativity in solitude and run his machinery with water power.

"Father was a hard guy to like," Esther admitted. She claims he was so domineering that the first 21 years of her life were totally tied up with him and his projects.

"He was his own doctor and thought he could carpenter better than anybody else, and he pretty near could. You could hardly find a chink in his armor," she conceded.

With Henry Ford and the assembly line as Frank's ideals, he put his entire family to work in his shop constructing his recently patented invention, the "Parker Nail Stripper," which became the family's main, and sometimes sole, source of income for years.

They also built wooden toys, little cradles and tables and chair sets for children, which they would bundle up and bring down to Wenatchee, where they would peddle them door-to-door.

Nineteen twenty-four began well enough. Spring came and a garden was planted. But just when the vegetables were all well started and promised a winter without hunger, a generation of ground hogs moved in and devoured the lot.

Their cow, strolling the ditch bank one day, fell into the water and drowned. The best thing about that bit of bad luck was that Frank allowed his family to eat the cow even though he had up to that point kept them all quite strictly vegetarian.

That fall when the toys were made, they crated and loaded them onto the lumber wagon for the trek to Wenatchee.

Esther's eight-year-old brother Frankie was sick that night. In the morning, three feet of untimely snow blanketed the world. They all grabbed shovels and began to clear some of it away from the wagon and to shovel paths to the barn and the shop. Suddenly, Frankie grabbed his head in pain, called out, and fell dead.

Charles, 14, and Glenn, 10, saddled two horses and rode three miles to the nearest phone to call the undertaker.

The depleted, grieving family eventually made their trip to the city; they HAD to go since they now had a funeral bill to pay. When they were just about ready to return home they received a call from the valley informing them their house had burned to the ground and everything was lost.

With the money they had made in Wenatchee they rented a garage in Winthrop and lived in it for a year.

"Everyone felt so sorry for us they held a dance for our benefit and gave us great big boxes of clothes," Esther said. "I washed and pressed them and cut them up and made them into new things. I was pretty bad at first, but I got better."

She certainly preferred sewing to working in her father's workshop. She had never had much material before but all of a sudden the community was supplying her with all the yardage she could use.

Dick McLean gave them a barrel of pickles and someone else gave them a side of beef.

That winter Esther almost died of measles, but she came through realizing she wasn't afraid of death.

"And I'm still not," she stated.

(August 1980)

Elmer and Aaron Johnson, On Work

This describes the way, the long way, three boys from the Methow Valley got to Seattle in 1912.

Aaron Johnson, 14, following a family tradition, ran away from home with an older brother. They spent two days and nights up on the hill behind the ranch living on a few raw potatoes they had brought along. The next night they spent hidden in the brush near the place and the fourth found them up Elbow Coulee, where they built a fire to keep warm. They connected up with a friend and the three started trudging down the valley. They walked as far as Methow, where the freight wagon lines had a station.

They had three cents between them so they sold a rifle to the wagon man for 50 cents to buy some cheese.

In Pateros they spent the night under a building.

From Pateros they walked and hitchhiked as far as Chelan, where they worked for 10 days on the Highline ditch. With their earnings they got to Wenatchee, where they hopped a freight train to Tacoma. They'd heard about berry picking near Puyallup but when Aaron got there he saw that "girls were doing the picking so that was out of my line." Instead, he got a job in a box factory on a machine that made cups for berries.

From there they went to Seattle, where Aaron got a job at Fisher's flour mill, a job he held for two years. Meanwhile, Aaron's brother and friend couldn't find work and were living with Aaron in a shack he was renting at six dollars a month. The three lived on the dollar a day Aaron made.

"Work," he said the other day, "it's just in me. You just go along, day by day, that's all there is to it."

He and his brother Elmer reminisce now that they're in their 70s.

Said Elmer, "People nowadays depend too much on other people. Old timers used to have to do all these things for themselves. I think work's good for a person. It never hurt anyone. I frankly think that leisure is harder on a person than work. Kids growing up today don't have any responsibilities; that's no good for them. It's not good to have things handed to you all the time."

Then Aaron spoke up. "They don't make worlds any better than this one, but when it comes to humans, we're not made as good. When I was young I could do anything in the world. I was high strung. But when your blood starts running cold you can't do what you used to."

Elmer always carried bacon rind whenever he drove anywhere in his Model T Ford. "I could fix my bearings with it," he explained. "That rind would hold everything together till I got home. It's about as tough as anything you can get a hold of."

He also knew how to gash the shoulders of cattle, shove in cloves of garlic, sew up the wounds with horse hair. This, he claimed, prevented black leg.

(June 1977)

Eulogizing Clara Williams

Clara Williams lived 82 of her 91 years in the Methow Valley, and she lived them to the hilt. Whatever came along, she was game. Many of those years she lived isolated up wild draws that define this land, accomplishing all the basics the hard way (the hard way being the only way things were done), and raising her 10 children on ingenuity.

Her general outlook might be summed up by what she said to me once in the Twisp Evergreen store in the aisle between the paper towels and the flapjack syrup. She said, "The world's just going to hell, ain't it? But you might as well see the bright side of things!"

I trust Heaven will be as absorbing for her as the Methow was. I have this vision of her approaching St. Peter. She walks straight up to the Heavenly Gates, which are wide open for her arrival. She takes a few steps inside and sweeps her gaze around the celestial spread and cries, "Well, I'll be! Isn't this the most amazing thing you ever saw!"

As far as I could tell, Clara never became what we normally think of as an old person. She met life head on and spoke her mind with such energy it made me wonder if she were a 23-year-old disguised as a 90-year-old.

One day, a few years back, Clara was pegging on down the sunny side of the street in Twisp, there between the Antlers Tavern and the auto parts store. She didn't know it, but a couple of friends of hers were sitting nearby in a car and heard the following exchange. A drunk weaved up to Clara and slurred, "Pardon me, Ma'am, but I'm a stranger in town. Do you happen to know where the liquor store is?"

She looked him straight in the eye and declared, "No, I don't. I'm a stranger here myself!"

What we say reflects what we are inside. It was Clara, so amazed at life, who was so amazing. All of us who knew her and loved her are far richer for having been blessed by that experience.

(From a eulogy given at the Senior Citizen Center in Twisp, March 21, 1987)

Johnny Klinkert, Miner

The Azurite Mine, spring of 1937.

Johnny Klinkert lay on his stomach in the dark raise, lighting the fuses with the flame from his carbide hat, careful not to let the spitting fuses blow out his fire. He had just finished drilling 27 holes and had placed seven sticks of dynamite in each one. The fuses varied in length, the longest six feet, the rest cut so that they would blast at the right time. A fuse burns about one foot a minute.

Johnny Klinkert

This particular tunnel was not only steep, but its bottom was filled with loose, wet muck. Another man was helping him that day, a farm boy from the Midwest who had never been underground before. He was not feeling at home down there.

The man was situated below John in the raise and had only nine fuses to light while John himself had eighteen. After they were lit, the plan was to go down 150 feet as quickly and carefully as possible and get to the level where they would ride out the blast.

That was the plan.

The man finished lighting his fuses before John, and all of a sudden he panicked and skedaddled as fast as he could. John heard the commotion and wheeled around. With horror, John watched as the loose muck started rolling behind the man.

The mudslide slurped down the incline, sealing the tunnel. And

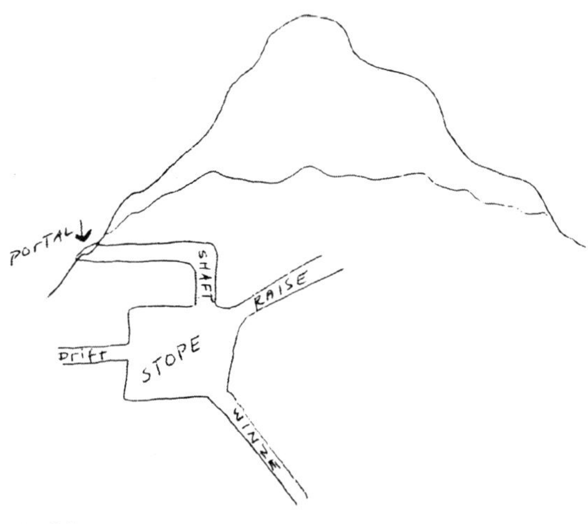

Azurite Mine

there was John with the fuses, burning steadily down.

“It got a little tense in there, and I’m not lying, “ John recalled.

Coolly, he finished lighting his fuses and then began scooping muck and gravel backwards with his hands. Fast. As he clawed his way along, he was happy that at least it was his legs, not his head, that were about to be blown to smithereens.

At the last minute his hands struck light. Hurling himself through the opening and swiveling around to gain purchase on the ladder, he descended 10 feet before the powder exploded. Rocks battered him as he pressed against the ladder.

Later, his shoulders were black and blue.

Despite this incident, John still, to this day, says, “You’re safer in a tunnel than you are out there on the street. Down in a tunnel you feel like you’re in God’s pocket.”

(January 1977)

Bill Robler, Rodeo Announcer

Bill Robler picked up a big leather megaphone. He hunkered down into an easy chair in the backroom of his house on Twisp's main street. The sound of the washing machine churned in the background. His tiny dog "Tiger" curled up on his lap.

The room began to fade as he looked directly into the past, and began.

"Hiya, folks, glad to see you this year. Hope we got enough entertainment to keep you occupied. If not, we'll have to put on something extry, like me getting bucked off this here cream-colored horse. First a few announcements...

"First rider out of the bareback chute is Foss Creveling. He's a good rider and he can jump off and land on his feet when his ride's done...

"First rider out of the saddle chute is "Ole" Scott on old Gravedigger. He's a hard ride, seldom been ridden...

"The next rider out of the saddle chute is Burt Evans from Timentwa, on Widowmaker...

"Next is Henry Mitchell. He's a good rider but you might have to sober him up to get him out here. Anyhow, he won the championship of the Northwest at the Pendleton Round Up. He's riding Black Cloud. And it's a good ride...

"Here comes bareback rider Boyd Eiffert on Pasayten Pete. He sure spins and twirls, so watch him, girls, see what he does. Well, he made a pretty good ride on him..."

Bill wasn't merely remembering, he was reliving the past. He began announcing for rodeos in Mansfield, Washington, in 1917 for C.B. Suzen's Wild West Show. As a sport, rodeoing was just getting a foothold in the country about that time.

Robler on his white horse "Buckles" became a familiar figure in rodeos around Brewster, Twisp, Winthrop, Chelan, Wapato Point, and Monse in the Big Bend country. With his strong voice and outgoing personality, he would ride 'round the arenas announcing the rides, making comments, keeping the crowd entertained and informed. In his angora chaps and beaded gloves, he would ride tall in the saddle and keep his mouth to the megaphone. When public address systems took over, Bill announced a few rodeos from the booth. But part of the show was lost when they unsaddled him and put him behind a microphone.

Calling for dances was another of Bill's talents. Dancing, too, was such an obsession with him that he and friends would go to any lengths to get to a dance.

He recalled rowing across the Columbia River, fighting off drifting ice to get to one. When they hit the other side, they hiked to the Morris schoolhouse. That night as they danced, a severe blizzard blew in and raged all night. They danced until five in the morning while the wind and snow howled outside, and then Mrs. Morris cooked everyone a huge breakfast of hotcakes, eggs and coffee, and the boys helped cut firewood and milk the cows. Then they all went back to the school, danced all day and all night and were finally able to row back across the river.

They had outdanced the blizzard.

(February 1977)

Ron McLean, Teacher

Ron McLean

For 20 years, Ron McLean taught first grade.

"I learned a lot from first graders," he admitted. A generation's first graders were lucky to have had Ron as their teacher. He was a listener, understanding things beyond the words, or lack of words. The children loved the lanky man who could be swayed to take his guitar off the hook on the wall beside the blackboard to sing to them about the rivers or friendly monsters or the coyotes in their backyards. He taught them about being human because he was so human, and he taught them to listen to one another.

Ron was generous with his talents as poet and balladeer of the Methow Valley. He said it best.

"Whatever it is a man must do
as the days of life pass by
must touch the lives of other men
or it's lost in the wind and the sky."

(From *The Hole in the Tall Gray Cliff*)

(December 1980)

Terry Fitzgibbons, Gambler

Terry Fitzgibbons

Terry Fitzgibbons was a gambling man. He dealt poker, blackjack, panguingue and threw dice for a living since the age of 17, when he first caught the fever. At 75 a deck of cards still looked right at home in his big hands.

"I'm just average," he lied about his poker-playing abilities, "but just like a carpenter, the longer you do it, the better you get."

Five-card stud was always Terry's game, a fact that sets him apart, points him out as a purist, a straight-shooter. "That's the greatest game a-goin'. Too much involved in a seven-card game, that's pretty hard to figure out; but if you play it scientific, five-card stud is best."

Terry was a regular in downtown Twisp in the backrooms and basements of the taverns where poker and dice games were avidly, and legally, played. He'd deal until morning for Stanley Nickell in the Antlers Tavern after he got off work at the mill at 1 a.m. He also dealt for Boyd Eiffert in his Club Cafe and got into big stakes pinochle games. Roving poker games in private houses were more the rule in Winthrop, although dice and cards at Three Fingered Jack's were not uncommon.

Terry never lost his touch, or his stash.

The best time in the valley for gambling was during hunting season, said Terry, when the saloons filled up with men in high spirits making the annual trip to the hills for the hunt and the gaming.

Terry, also a good hunter, liked to spend time up in the mountains going after bear or deer, staying in cabins in the wilderness and taking part in a friendly game after the sun went down.

He plunked his winnings into fishing boats or new cars, a different one every year. He didn't save much of his take and ended up living on Social Security.

At least he didn't have to support anyone else. He never married.

"Nope," he said good-humoredly. "I never did. People don't get married nowadays, do they?" he joked. "What's the use of it, anyway?"

Terry ended his days down at the Twisp Garden Apartments. Not in terrific health, he read a lot, and once in awhile he'd fondly pick up a nice new deck of slippery cards and deal himself out a quiet game of solitaire.

(June 1981)

Howard and Ressie Wellers' Snapshots

The photographs tell stories about their lives they forget to verbalize. Details tend to get lost in the outline of 50 full years together.

The 8x10 glossies offer glimpses of early logging in the valley when the trees were many feet thick and shaggy-hoofed work horses lined up sullenly for their picture before a day of skidding the monster logs through the woods. Other photos show a young, confident Howard Weller, supervisor of logging and road construction, standing by the boulders his men and machines bulldozed away to create mile after mile of county roads up numerous valleys and side creeks.

Then there are the tiny snapshots, eight to a small page. Here's Ressie, a young girl on her wedding day, with a spit curl on her forehead. As their lives progressed together, the years offer different poses, different scenes, and children appear, one two three four.

Pictures of the flood of '48 are wedged in between family and friends, and then you come to one of Howard crawling through deep snow in the mountains. There's a long story goes with that one, as there are endless memories connected with each one.

The triggered memories belong to Howard and Ressie Weller, who will be married 50 years come this July.

(April 1979)

Guy Vintin, Rancher

Guy Vintin

Heading east out of Carlton, winding up the dirt road past sage and Ponderosa, the green swatch of bottomland along the river disappears in the folds of the dry, seemingly inhospitable foothills. This land once lay buried under hundreds of feet of blue glacier during the Ice Age.

Despair could come easily to the fainthearted in such terrain. But suddenly the land springs to life: alfalfa and head-high corn burst from the stubborn soil, yanked out only by one thing: unrelenting work.

The road stops dead between the sheds of machinery, the collapsing root cellar, the barn glutted to the eaves with hay and stacks of hundreds of more bales outside, and the old weathered home of Guy Vintin and his three sons, Dave, Gene, and Tom.

Known all over the Methow as the Vintin Brothers, the three sons carry on a tradition of work during hay and corn harvest that would stagger most mortals conditioned to the eight-hour day.

"Eight hours? What's that?" demanded Guy, 91-year-old patriarch of Vintin Road. "Three o'clock in the morning until 10 at night, now THAT was a day's work when I was riding the range. We didn't know what overtime was, them days.

"I used to think I was quite a man," he rasped. "I could put a hundred fifty pound wheat sack over my head. Now I can't even lift twenty." At almost 92, one should be allowed such failings. After all, he broke every bone on the left side of his body and two on his right during his lifetime camaraderie with horses and cattle.

"An old guy told me soon after we'd moved here in 1940 that we'd never leave the Methow Valley because we'd never get enough money," he said. It's been 40 years since the prophet's words.

For the past six years Guy wintered in California with his daughter and his grandchildren. He would walk them to school in the morning, holding their hands and crossing the streets together. The children trusted this man who had galloped the open hills and rounded up wild horses, who held a thousand reins and plowed a straight line.

Guy admitted the only thing he would change in his life had he the chance to live it over again would be to eliminate all the broken bones.

(September 1980)

Jim Abel, Cowboy

Jim Abel, cowboy of the old school, doesn't put up with swearing around women, keeps his head and his own counsel, treats his animals right, and talks to them when he has something to say.

" 'Star, old girl,' I said to her the other day, 'we're both growing old together.' " Jim, 60, talks to Star a fair amount, since he spends a good deal of time with her out in the hills. He and Star have 300 head of cattle to keep track of up Boulder Creek.

Star, at 14, is one peach of a cowhorse. You can tell Jim thinks the world of her.

"My dad once told me, 'You'll only have one good horse in a lifetime.' Well, I've had five," he said, struck by such uncalled-for privilege.

What sort of thoughts go through Jim's head as he's being carried on Star's back up the dusty trails through pine shadow, through dancing water, hour after hour, lighting cigarette after cigarette, keeping his practiced eye peeled for signs of strays?

"Where's that g... d.... cow!?" That's what.

Jim has had a long, fruitful association with the animal world. He grew up around horses, spent years packing for the Forest Service, and worked with just about every packer in this valley. He probably spent a lot of time talking to milk cows, too, since he was only six when he was introduced to that occupation.

He "broke eight head of cows to milk" when he was just a kid and has spent most of his life in barns.

Jim treats animals right because horses, mules and cows don't talk back, they don't yell at you or tell you what to do. He puts a lot of stock in being his own boss, keeping his own hours, throwing back a shot of whiskey and a chaser of beer when he feels like it.

"It's never been written down any place drinking and riding don't mix. I'd've frozen to death many times hadn't been for whiskey," he said, straightening out any misconceptions on that score.

The act of drinking fits in with the old school of working with animals, of putting in long hours in cold and heat and darkness. His hands are getting bad, he says, uncoiling them imperfectly from around the comforting curve of a shot glass. He tells how his hands froze so hard they

Jim Abel

couldn't light a match after splitting wood because of chainsawing cattle trail in the raw spring and sudden fall cold and wrapping ice-stiff tarps around heavy supplies and tying unwieldy loads with frozen rope.

Mules' flanks weren't the only warmth around at times like those. There was often that instant head-blooming warmth from a slug of whiskey.

So how do cowboys like Jim fit into the 20th century? Ignoring it is Jim's way. Besides, he thinks cowboying will always be like he's known it.

"You can't just push a button and get those cows to come out of the hills. You'll always have to have an old horse, and if you've got one, a good dog to move those cows," he explained.

If the technological age should ever cancel out campfires, where will the Jim Abels of the world turn for cheer and warmth in that ink black of wilderness nights? What other time and place sets the scene so well for tall tales and a cup of something good resting in overworked hands?

He doesn't worry himself over such matters.

He noted, "Bankers got ulcers. I don't."

When the subject of retirement came up, he said, "I'll retire only when I can't get on a horse anymore." He paused. A light sparked his eyes. "Guess I'm going to have to get smaller and smaller horses."

He nodded approval of that original notion and took a satisfied pull from the smooth amber liquid in his glass.

(September 1984)

Chapter III

Opinionated Pen

Voices stand out in a place where the beating of your heart is often the loudest sound within hearing. Because they're heard, people use their voices, and opinions proliferate like barnaby thistle. Outspokenness is the most common trait around.

Ruth Davis, known for her definite stand on every subject, declared, "I've seen a lot of changes in this valley, and I'm agin every one of them." Since she moved here in 1895, she must have spent a good portion of her decades here being "agin" one thing or another.

When I was offered the heady opportunity to express myself on the editorial pages of the local newspaper, I felt free to wing my comments out into the public. No one ever scorned me for any of my outbursts. They simply went with the territory.

Promises, Promises

I'm not a spoiler by nature: I'll champion accomplishments, all acts of true bravery, and opportunities grabbed and run with.

However, I do tend to be skeptical about promises, and in particular promises made to the Methow Valley supposedly on the valley's behalf.

The valley has a long list of broken promises attached to its history, starting at the turn of the century when talk about a railroad being built through the area filled years worth of Methow Valley Newses back when Harry Marble edited the paper. The railroad was going to put the valley on the map.

But the tracks got laid elsewhere. The valley got bypassed, up until 10 years ago, that is, when the North Cascades Highway opened the place to the multitudes.

Visitors and passers-by, struck by the all-too-apparent qualities of the Methow, are coming to a screeching halt here and claiming the place as if it were their own personal discovery.

More and more promises are being made by more and more people, and some of them are being broken before our very eyes. Remember Fort Fun? What happened to the high frequency radio tower scheduled for Mazama? Where's the story of Aspen going? Who can even count all the stores that opened their doors with high hopes, then silently closed them after a few months?

The valley has not yet broken Rick Miller.

Something Rick said struck me as being honest in its appraisal of the valley and honest to his own absolute vision. He said, "The valley is a very, very rough place to live.
I see no hope for this valley but my dehydrator. It could increase people's standard of living by a quarter."

Rick is a man of vision. Maybe his vision will withstand the ravages of the Methow winter and maybe it won't. It bears watching, certainly.

Thank goodness there are people who swear by their insights: we'd be a sorry country without them (the people and the insights). Rick's dehydrator might indeed be the answer to the economic calamity of this valley, and then again maybe it's just another cold wind blowing down from the peaks.

Time will tell. Meanwhile, be skeptical about promises. The history of the valley continues to be made by us, here, now.

(October 1981)

Epilogue: Rick's idea was just another cold wind blowing down from the peaks.

Community Blood

As I lay hip to hip with Tom Whatsisname from the road department, head to his feet, my feet to his head, on the hard pad, in the U-shaped "station," a needle in my arm, the bag filling with my red-black blood, I heard in that strangely quiet gym set up for blood-letting, muffled yelling emanating from two transistor radios.

It was the yelling of the crowd at the state girls' basketball tournament being fought 175 miles away.

As I was halfway through donating my pint, our team lost. I suddenly felt the resignation in the gym as the community readjusted itself to the disheartening news.

I then started wondering if the lack of our usual crowd during our twice-annual blood giving had been due to the new AIDS plague. But the Red Cross has devised an ingenious way in which a person in a community as small as ours can actually go all the way through the process of donating tainted blood and walk out a free man, never having to implicate himself. What he does is merely check a secret box saying, destroy my blood, let it go no farther.

I realized later the reason for the slashed numbers this particular day had been due to the exodus of carloads of fans flowing away from this remoteness to that far city where our high school girls had played their hearts out hard enough to get that far. Thus the quietness when the two transistors were snapped off and placed beneath the metal chairs, and the almost audible readjustment back to our lives without the glory we'd envisioned.

Still, we let our blood for use God knew where – maybe we'd need it sometime – I know I had, once, one scary time, pints and pints of it. I would have died, otherwise. It happened within three months of moving to this community. Because this had happened, I learned this was a place that looked after its own, with concern. People dropped by. I was weak. They brought bread, and a shy welcome. That was 15 years ago.

So, there we were in the grade school gym, bleeding into plastic bags. We had been processed, answered a lot of personal questions, chatted, laughed, made jokes with everyone around us, lain cheek to jowl or foot to head, with our pharmacist, our ex-editor, our Italian teacher, our husband's school colleague, our mechanic, our yoga instructor, our favorite restaurant owner, our septic-tank siphoner, our neighbors (five miles in both directions), our hairdresser, all of us bleeding happily together.

Then volunteers – whom we know from casual but constant meetings on streets and in stores – take our elbows gently and lead us over to the grade school refectory table where we stuff our faces with triangular sandwiches and cookies, and Eagles Auxiliary ladies ask if we want coffee, tea, or milk, then slap a sticker on our chests that reads, "Be nice to me, I gave blood today." We smile, and wear it out to the grocery store before going home, hoping one of the clerks will notice.

Not that it matters. We've done our bit, lain cheek to jowl, or foot to head, with our community, and heard our girls cheered over scratchy radios as our communal blood flowed.

That's community. There's no substitute.

(April 1987)

A Walk to Town

Last week a day dawned that epitomized the best of Methow autumn: dazzling, pure, pungent, with a November sun as warm as it could be in such a latitude. I burst outdoors and wanted to stay there forever.

Since I had to go to town, I decided to walk the five miles down the Twisp River Valley. As I strode eastward, I saw and felt something different from what I had before: that as diverse as all of us were who lived along the road, as concerned as we were about one or two things in particular, we functioned as a community. We lived, to put it crudely, to service each other.

I saw: Jehovah's Witnesses out in their turquoise station wagon making their appointed rounds, spreading the Word as they read it; PUD rigs parked under power poles ready to scale to high voltage pinnacles; Joe Setting rushing to the elementary school to fix the furnace; the plumber out on call; woodcutters armed with chain saws, German shepherds and friends headed into the hills to cut a cord or two before snowfall.

I passed the houses of carpenters, teachers, medical technicians, waitresses.

The community in microcosm passed me as I ambled down valley, observing the servers, those concerned with our souls, our power sources, our plumbing, our education, our health, our homes and our nourishment.

No member of any tribe could have felt as secure as I did. I felt more at home than ever.

(November 1981)

Downtown

I've always been impressed with how much one can do on the mere two-and-a-half blocks of downtown Twisp. Listing those things gives me an almost perverse pleasure. Permit me.

On the main street of Twisp you can get: a piston, a divorce, an ice-cream cone, a new wardrobe, a haircut, drunk, groceries, a story in the paper, a skein of yarn, arrested, a registered letter, a pizza, a ceramic cat, gas, breakfast-lunch-dinner, a postage-due letter, mud flaps, a gold filling, a lube job, bifocals, a double-bitted axe, insurance, your TV fixed, chicken feed, into a good conversation over coffee, pipe, Clorox, a sunburn, your meat out of your freezer locker, into a fender-bender. You can also go to a movie, play Pac-man, deposit your pay check, learn how to tat, go to a town council meeting, meet your friends and your enemies.

Downtown Twisp can occupy your lifetime. Or you can close your eyes and stride the length of it in a minute-and-a-half.

(March 1982)

Six Minutes in Twisp

It's Thursday morning in downtown Twisp: 8:23 by the ONB clock. I'm sitting on the bench in front of the post office in the feeble sunshine. The American flag snaps half-heartedly in a soft breeze. One of last fall's leaves scrapes along the sidewalk and holds my attention for a while. Behind the bank, in a back yard, clothes swing back and forth from a line.

8:24. Thursday has yet to start throbbing.

8:25. I turn my head and watch a man a block away, thumbtacking a notice on the one wood building in town that escaped the Great Fire of '24. It's now the town's bulletin board. There's where we learn about yard sales, religious revivals, upcoming dances, whereabouts of auctions.

Dan's probably already snipping a customer's conservative thatch; the barber pole's revolving at 8:26. The double-duty clock also tells me it's 46 degrees. The sun's doing its job, though.

No noise mars the perfection of 8:27. The leaf has scuttled as far as my foot. I know that behind me in the post office, scores of chicks are cheeping in their cardboard cartons. I can see them stacked. I heard them yesterday.

Another thing I know is, in these hills that loom up over the rooftops of our town, minuscule spring wildflowers are swaying and deer are ambling, and crows are teasing coyotes.

8:29, a car drives by, Larry going down to the cafe to join the boys for coffee.

Our town wakes up slowly as an old woman who's sure of herself, with no doubt in her mind she'll get done what has to be done, in her own sweet time.

(May 1985)

Say, Molly, Where's Fifth Avenue?

Signs tacked up on town bulletin boards invite everyone to gigantic, tantalizing yard sales.

Problem is, when an address is given, most people don't have the foggiest notion where most of the streets are in Twisp.

Do YOU know where Days Lane is? How about Alder? Fifth Avenue? Riverside Avenue? Marble Street?

Did you know there's Second, Third, Fourth and Fifth Avenue in Twisp but no First Avenue? First Avenue is called Twisp Avenue, and after crashing into a rubble bank, it's called Borchard Lane.

There's a family, whose name shall remain secret, that has lived on a particular street for 25 years. The daughter (18 years old) didn't have a clue what it was called, and her mother had to think twice before dredging up North Johnson. If that's North Johnson, South Johnson must be that slash of dirt near the tennis courts where Igor the Can Crusher lives.

Mike Fisher has had a business on a back street for years but he has no idea what it's called. (Lincoln, Mike.) You either know where he works or you call him. His business card, if he had one, would read: "Mike Fisher, Mobile Mechanic, near the fire house. Find me if you can."

One thing is certain, you don't have to be dead in this town before a street's named after you. There's a Marie Street up on the plateau near the grade school named after Marie Risley. One evening, years ago, the Twisp Town Council, of which she was a member, was sitting around naming streets. Everyone liked her name, and besides, she'd been born in Twisp in 1903. Marie Street, by the way, is near Harrison, Bigelow and Painter streets.

Ernest and Danny Days' homes are the only two houses on Days Lane. Olive Johnson lives on North Johnson. The Dan Doran family lives on Doran Drive. Oral Magers lives on Magers Street.

Main street down the center of town is not called Main Street. It's called Glover. Before Twisp was incorporated, the place was called Gloversville.

Back around 1950 some Boy Scouts carved and painted street signs for the town. A few are still tacked up, but some you have to get out of your car to read because they're so faded, and a few face the wrong direction.

Other signs were affixed not long ago, but someone in an odd frame of mind removed them and heaved them over the bank into the Methow River at the foot of Canyon Street, if you know where that is.

Part of Twisp's charm is that it hasn't quite made a concession to the 20th century yet. But let's face it, times are changing and the town is no longer one big extended family. It's even gotten to the point that firemen and policemen (some of them newcomers) are getting baffled by, "Quick, the Carr's house is burning down," rather than, "Quick, 124 Hagerman Street's burning down."

(June 1985)

Rambling (on and on) to Twisp

Nice sunny September morning to walk to town I feel ready to STRIDE OUT five miles no sweat. Funny how from the road I look at our sprawl of land as if it were someone else's flying over the fields up the back 40 into the trees up to the ridge. Here come Rex and Otto loud barkers ready to run me off their part of the globe. Haha! Rex! Otto! I'm your neighbor, silly dogs. They're an odd looking pair, like lots of pairs. Flume Grade rising into the sunshine – seems late for the ditch to be running so full spilling lustily down the spillway I'm practically free-flying it's so steep here. Hope I don't fall on my ass walking backwards but I've got to say 'bye to Reynolds Peak. Why don't cars ever hurtle over this cliff? Pat and Chris Christianson's fields look fine, as usual fertile, harvest-ready, neat. I see Norm and Fern Reynaud have stuffed their loaf-like barn full of alfalfa once more. God it's quiet up here today where's that melodious cricket singing? I'm glad people have finally learned not to stop and ask me if I want a ride, unless my thumb's in the air. There's the loveliest vision along the route, Poorman Creek Valley swooping up to Hoodoo. Second Mile Ranch was an interesting experiment in Christian living I wonder would those folks call it a success or a failure. This S-curve sure isn't scary when you're walking what's everyone doing in their houses along orchard flats this morning? Structures of mystery, every one. Earl Jones' s honking geese remind me of some other country Hi, Earl! Hi, Elmer. Elmer Johnson's paying a neighborly visit that's nice. Too bad about Durocher's lush hay crop cut the day the rains started. What's Terry Kinder doing these days? Probably working his way to the Presidency, I hope. Have they started picking apples up in King's orchard God I hated it when the little twigs caught my hair I was an awful picker much too slow who's that talking up by the ditch where Perry Brewster grows hay I can almost hear their words from here. There's Dick Cardinal bringing salt blocks down to his cattle their painted mailbox is flaking and the bird's gone Hi, cows. Where's the colt that mare had last spring? Boy this is great striding down Spokane Grade my knee functioning perfectly again how I envied people who could walk along THROWING THEIR LEGS OUT in front of them without a thought left right left right jeez this hill scares me on icy days the roadbed sure looks like it slants toward the cliff no wonder I instinctively brake. They call this Little Siberia but the shadows feel nice today though when you drive fast into the shadesunshadesun it feels like being in a strobe light. Hey here're pussy willow bushes they sure look dull with leaves on what's that purple throated pigeon doing strolling along on the other side of the road. Up hill entering city limits slow down past the police chief's house Whoa! as Ross Filer says when we come to a stop sign. Ross' door is padlocked he must be at the Branding Iron which he calls the Hoot Owl. Harry Eiffert taught me there's a speed limit here when he stopped me I says Harry, I've been speeding here for twelve years I wonder why I say the wrong things so often? At least I slow down now. Who's at the clinic today, anyone I know? I wonder where that small blue ambulance is I rode in back in '73? New one's a mobile emergency room. Kindergarten must be letting out lots of mothers coming down the gradeschool hill with little bodies beside them. Here's town and I have no aches. Think I'll mosey into the Branding Iron for a once-through on Rosey's salad bar. Hachoo! Whoops. Folks, I did NOT sneeze into the salads! (I wonder if they believe me?) Thank goodness for sneeze guards.

(October 1985)

Nannied to Death

Big Brother's trying to put us all to sleep.

There I was, tooling along around 50 mph, thinking about 17 things at once, when my foot automatically sidestepped over to the brake pedal.

Coming up on a one-lane bridge means you have to calculate. You have to look to see if anyone's coming, you have to decide if you can shoot on through, or if you should stop and let the other car drive over first. Slowed or stopped, you always see the river below, greeny and jumpy over the rocks.

But my foot braked me for nothing. The one-laner had been replaced by a sail-on-over type.

I felt cheated. I had just been deprived of exercising judgment. I was offended I'd been denied my right to fend for myself, to exercise a little humanity.

Big Brother's turning us into spiritual paupers. He slaps so many safety codes, regulations, and cautionary instructions on us, our judgment is going to wither away. We're being anesthetized by overprotection. We're being nannied to death.

While journeying to Africa I became aware that the reason I felt so AWAKE was because no one coddled me, no one pretended they cared for my safety. I had to learn to read the danger signs on my own. Survival alone was exhilarating. Risk-taking was daily fare.

I feel insulted by those signs that have just been put up in the last few years that read, "Primitive Road No Warning Signs." Holy moley, does that mean I'm going to have to figure out all by myself how fast to go around the corner? Can I manage it?

When I discovered I wouldn't have to brake for the Weeman Bridge any more, it brought back into perspective how many ways we're being protected "for our own safety." It's killing us. How long will it be before we won't know how to perform even the simplest act of survival because we've not been allowed to exercise our own powers of judgment for so long?

(May 1985)

Inhuman Eye of the Government

It was recently announced that the Forest Service would no longer require entry permits into the wilderness.

Frankly, I never got them. I figured it was none of anyone's business if I'd decided to slip into the wilderness for a few days of peace.

I hated having someone come up to me two days into the mountains to snoop around my campfire, check my garbage habits, see I had a permit to be where I was. It was downright Orwellian.

The information gathered, we are informed, was used to "PROVIDE PEOPLE QUALITY WILDERNESS EXPERIENCES."

Wrong! It cannot do this! Quality wilderness experiences are provided, not by the Forest Service, but by the mountains, the air, our own souls in solitary relation to the surroundings.

They go on. "It's no longer essential" (it never was) "that we so closely track" (one tracks down beasts to kill) "visitor activities in the wilderness." (My activities in the wilderness included actively pursuing solitude; I did not go into the wilds to be tracked down by my government.)

I resented needing a permit to be alone. When they were required and I didn't get them, I was made to feel like an outlaw. Now that these won't be required, what's next on the government's agenda so it can keep its inhuman eye on us?

(June 1985)

Dreams that Crash

I'm struck by the number of dreams that go crash in the Methow, how people arrive bristling with grandiose ideas that, some sooner, some later, become brief footnotes to this valley's history.

I've done several lengthy, glowing articles about those brainstorms: drying herbs on a grand scale, running camps for the disabled, making the Methow over into a retreat center, a health resort, a heart rehabilitation mecca, a downhill ski Chamonix, a degenerative disease research complex. Businesses too numerous to list have flunked, folded, disappeared.

Amidst all this flux a few endeavors endure, like farming, ranching, logging (the failed mill is another story, based on national economics); certain cafes, most churches, all taverns, a few longstanding stores, the Forest Service, schools, gas stations, and real estate agencies, are all more or less essential so they live on.

It makes me think the Methow Valley accommodates what it can naturally support. Bursting enthusiasm and idealism often get tempered by the valley's cold, heat, dryness, lack of general interest or lack of population. As a local wise man assessed, it takes honesty to last here.

Honesty in this context entails perhaps something like this: dry-eyed perspective on your own talents and adaptability and on the valley's real need for what you've got to offer.

The place is not full of pioneers anymore. They're dying out. Their time's done. We're in a period of transition; the valley's being leased by a whole new generation made up of people abandoning the fast-paced, computerized world, and some who think they're getting in on the ground floor of a boom area.

Pioneers possessed the strength born of having lived through generally harder years with no "conveniences." They knew and practiced discipline; they didn't borrow money. They hadn't been undermined by the glittery dictates of advertising or by the debilitating backdrop of annihilation. Their brain cells hadn't been put on the fritz by computers or its jargon, hadn't gone fuzzy around the edges by too much media blast. They called spades spades and called it a day when the sun went down.

I'm singing a song to the past. Unfortunately, it's behind us. We're writing new history in this valley. It remains to be seen which dreams take hold.

(October 1983)

Letting Go

My privilege to say goodbye in this editorial space compels me to bow to those who, over the years, have allowed me to record the stories of their lives, lives shaped on the anvil of early Methow Valley pioneering.

They, with brave trust, offered me glimpses into the sacred domain of their private actions over a lifetime, granted me the terrifying freedom to find an outline, and lay bare the findings in this newspaper.

With growing enthusiasm, I became the willing instrument in "untangling the plot in the play," as Malcom Cowley describes the act of trying to find a shape or pattern in one's life, in his book, "The View From 80."

Collectively, the stories formed a mosaic of the history of the valley; individually, each article praised a generation passing from our ken; personally, the process gave rebar to my soul, bequeathing me a center which will hold as I wander beyond the comfort barriers of the Methow.

They have answered a thousand questions, have taught me the worth of a long life in one place, have taken me on as a friend. They have spoiled me for any other livelihood or any other home.

I'll miss that elation kindled by having pages of notes ready to gather into an article: a banty must feel the same way brooding on a nest of eggs, full of promise. If the results are mixed, the intent at least was pure.

In case all this sounds terminal, let me hasten to say that I leave for a mere 14 months and intend to take up the same work on my return. Because I go to Africa, the image of leaving seems to complicate into a certain foreboding, but life here, I know, can be equally tenuous. Some of you may not be here when I get back.

Don't think it takes courage to travel in such foreign lands: genuine courage is between almost every line in the pioneers' stories.

I'm not ungrateful, I trust, or unaware of the paradise I leave behind. Travel is a
quirky lust that strikes and must be heeded, if only to pay a moving tribute to the place one settles.

(June 1982)

We're Home

We're home. Returning after circling the globe for nearly 14 months, Bill and I are being greeted so warmly by everyone that the meaning of "home" has been defined for me all over again.

Home is where the barriers are down; where you don't have to constantly explain who you are; where the smiles are alive with recognition; where the bonds between people have been so tempered with years of varied experiences they're almost visible.

There's one question everyone asks: How does it feel being back in the valley? I think the underlying question is, How does the valley compare with the rest of the world?

All right, I'll say. Even though I grade the Methow Valley A+, I'd be less than honest if I gave the impression that there aren't places we saw that could be considered more beautiful, more fertile, more intriguing, and populated with more friendly people than here.

There are.

But, you see, THIS is home. Where I thrive. Where you thrive. Where the welcomes are so real I ache.

Several times during our long journey the valley was my mental refuge. Times I felt alien, far from comfort, lonely for a familiar face, I sat beneath the maple in our back yard, or stood in cottonwoody shade beside the Twisp River, or went my way up the curving road beside the Methow River from Pateros through those dry hills. I ushered up the valley's spaces, smells and sounds, peopled the houses with friends. In short, I envisioned home.

The transition from journey to home has been ecstatic. A friend grew us a garden; others have called up, stopped by, rolled out the red carpet. And I'm not stringing anyone along when I say the water that falls from our taps, so freely and so cold, is the sweetest water anywhere. Period.

We're home, in one piece, and even though I don't pretend to know how the universe is run, our safe and healthy return may very well be due to all of you who wished us well throughout the year.

(August 1983)

Litany of Things Forgotten

I knew the insights would never last. They seldom do. Like springtime or youth, the life cycle of an insight is never long enough.

I've been home in the Methow for a year after spending the previous year mostly in Third World countries. I came back determined not to forget what I'd seen.

But now, though I'm not much fatter, I forget for weeks on end the look of hunger. I've also forgotten the look of bureaucrats thriving on bribery, and nature as the wild taker and giver of life. I've forgotten the debilitating irritation of poison insects and ubiquitous flies, unstoppable heat and thirst, unmaintained vehicles bearing me shatteringly over non-roads.

I've forgotten the distances people travel on foot to find enough sticks to burn to cook the next few meals, while I pile branches off the trail. I only take the big stuff. If they could see the wood I toss, they'd die of ecstasy to be so near it.

I've forgotten the heart-breaking care a man gave to a few lettuce leaves. He lived in the Sahara where rain never has fallen. Here, outside my door, my lush garden explodes with row upon row of fat vegetables.

This valley has a way of tampering with my visions of elsewhere. Rivers run pure, the soil is fertile, seasons follow each other with few surprises. Since I've seen its opposite, I know the Methow is as close to Heaven as most people in the world can imagine. But this beauty and fecundity, especially at this time of year, is blotting out my memory. I lie on dazzling grass in the evening reading a book and forget to mentally bow to those who have never seen the likes of that grass or known the ease I've known all along.

I fear I'm beginning to think this is normal, somehow my due.

But it's not. Not at all.

(July 1984)

Monastery Road

The way I figure it, it can only be done alone. I wedge one of those large Styrofoam cups brimming with Duck Brand coffee into the handy seatside holster, throw the throttle into forward, and head west.

Solitary tripping over the North Cascades Highway has become for me – no matter what the journey's purpose – an end in itself. It's not the scenery, although it forms the decoration on the walls of my heart and mind as I move through that sanctum.

The curvaceous, 40 mph road up the valley floor past Heath's herds, the Jesus-fearing Bible camp, and old homesteads leads me inexorably into myself. Coffee's drunk by Klipchuck, so as soon as Silver Star stabs the sky on the left my thoughts are riding me like wild stallions. Liberty Bell often doesn't exist, and Whistler whistles past in a green blur too high beyond my right window's vision. By Rainy Pass I'm having improbable conversations with myself, sometimes in French. I'm a hero, a victim, I'm passionate, I never die. I glimpse Ross Lake, but since I have the scenery memorized it makes no impression except to inform me of my progression in generally the right direction. Last time over, somewhere near Diablo, I sat down beside my mother. She's been dead eight years, but it wasn't until that fierce road beside the Skagit before Newhalem that I truly missed her.

The smell of wetness (and the bewildering sound of dripping) is often enough to bring me back to my senses. Cast in Methow dryness, I find the odor of juicy vegetation brings on mild states of ecstasy. By Marblemount's Mountain Song Restaurant I begin bowing out of the chapel of my heart. The elation in my soul deflates as words are spoken. "Tahini dressing, please," seems to break the spell. Yet one rainfall between Rockport and Darrington, down that long corridor of dark, weeping trees, I flipped on the radio thinking myself able to hear something else. Suddenly strange music catapulted me right back into my reverie.

Interstate 5 always kills it for me. It's speed and faceless thousands barreling along behind glaring windshields and it terrifies me. I'm all nerves, and for miles it's impossible to reconcile this sudden onslaught of humanity with the sanctuary I've visited thus far.

By Seattle, the coffee's worn off completely, the emotions have faded. I have a few scrawled notes, an empty, ugly cup, and a glow somewhere so deep I can't get at it. Time for a movie.

(May 1986)

Route 153

If brochures ballyhooing the Cascade Loop waste few words on Route 153, a sinuous 30-mile segment that leaps the Methow River nine times between Twisp and Pateros, perhaps it's because 153 doesn't cough up enough spectacles. After driving out from between 8,000 footers on the North Cascades Highway, to roll south along this hiatus valley road is like straying into someone's backyard.

It's hard ignoring a suspicion that nature and topography don't coddle the valley's inhabitants. Woodpiles like barricades tell of winters so hard apple trees have popped and died. Summer's so hot even the river offers scant respite from the thirsty air. If homes along the route fail to meet Better Homes and Gardens standards, that's because folks seldom strike it rich here. In fact, some families have hung around for generations trying to yank life from the soil, unable to earn enough cash to skedaddle.

Heading south, the road plays warp to the river's woof, weaving a hectic rug of fields and orchards that imperfectly covers the flatlands. The valley, broadening and narrowing between sagey, rocky foothills, presents periodic glimpses of the stagecoach trail hacked into its lower flanks east of the river. Tiny towns hunch beside the road every 11 miles or so – the mean distance a horseman cared to be in the saddle before needing a cup of coffee. Each town, technically speaking, is about the size of three deep breaths taken while driving the speed limit. It takes some vigilance to not miss them.

Twisp (population 900), in contrast to its false-fronted neighbor to the north, is the Methow Valley's main working town, pretending nothing else. Hang a left at the Chevron station and take it in, all two blocks of it. Lots of grass and the shade of scattered ponderosa make for fine picnicking in the city park at the confluence of the Twisp and Methow rivers, just down the hill from the Antlers Tavern.

At 40 mph, perfect rubbernecking speed (and easier on your reflexes if mule deer cross the road or if your eye snags on an eagle), you approach Carlton, capital of the winter cribbage tournament held beside the wood stove in the general store. It's possible to miss the town if your mind wanders at this point; nevertheless, Carlton sports an establishment called Major Collision.

If side roads entice, a dozen of them make gravelly dashes into side valleys. Get a map or take potluck up Squaw, Texas, Gold, French, Benson, or Libby. They'll take you a) absolutely nowhere; b) to the ridge of the Sawtooth Range; or c) to mountain lakes.

After playing leapfrog with the river, the road snuggles beside it a ways before swooping upon the unincorporated town of Methow, home of Mike's (defunct) Market and a reputation for keeping its Christmas decorations hanging on the main telephone pole until August. A cafe, usually open, serves trout spawned on a farm a few miles away.

From here to the Columbia River, apple orchards, some sprouting on Incaic plateaus, bristle everywhere. At Route 153's terminus the Methow River slows and splays, all the wild taken out of it, and obliterates itself in the placidified Columbia. Pateros, sprawled along the banks of both rivers, was bulldozed down 20 years ago when Azwell Dam raised the water's level. More than half the population stomped away mad, and sad. Today, it's mostly the Apple Pie Jamboree the third weekend of July that seduces folks to the town, although Pateros' distinction as a prime steelhead fishing hole is starting to bait hundreds of fishermen.

(May 1986)

Wonder

If I paid more attention, I'd get positively shaky about this unsettling century of ours.

For example. Last week I spent the night in someone else's house and found myself alone with an incredible machine: a satellite-connected TV. As my finger touched a cold rectangular piece of steel, numbers beamed greenly electronic up at me. Outside among the snow-sheathed barnaby thistle I could sense the dish turning its blank face toward Aurora, Galaxy, Comstar, Westar, Anik and Telstar. Houston Bible beaters, naked women transponding, Gary Cooper and Mexican sitcoms all flashed by on the screen. I slept fitfully on the floor in front of it and it hummed to me even though I thought I'd turned the thing off.

Next morning I headed home, walking the three miles, in and out of little valleys cold in sunshine and shade. Fifteen deer scaled a hill in front of me with enviable dignity, then they sensed me, and like that dish the night before, their ears rotated on their heads, picking up my vibrations and other signals. They scooted off to deer land beyond human vision and I made home.

Home is where no push-button furnace automatically keeps the temperature at the comfort zone, so I took up the double-headed axe and sliced neat lengths of frigid fir and turned them into heat in the wood stove. As the kettles began to purr, the telephone rang and I heard my sister speaking to me from 3,000 miles away. Even though her words flew over West Virginia and Illinois and Nebraska and Montana to land in my ear, no pause existed between her speaking them and my hearing them.

After the call I punched a button and Louis Armstrong sang to me. He and his band played Dixieland for me, and somehow all those horns and drums were emanating off a piece of flimsy plastic with no marks of any kind on it.

I skied down to the cabin to split wood for a guest coming for the weekend. Halfway there I stopped on the blinding field and in the silence I heard my blood coursing through my veins, a sound so elemental, it wiped out thought.

Later, I got into the pickup and transported myself in a sitting position past farms and fields to town. A voice spoke to me over the mountains in Omak about the election in the Philippines. I spent the next couple of hours plunking away on my banjo while older people danced, and as they glided by me I'd remember how one had come here by stagecoach, another had broken virgin soil in this valley with horses. I wondered what my friends and I would dance to when we got old. I wondered if we'd all be traveling instantaneously by stepping into a machine that would turn us into atoms and blow us to, say, Afghanistan, in microseconds, where we'd be reconstituted.

I walked across the street to the post office and in my mailbox found a letter from a friend living on an island hardly anyone's ever heard of. It got from the Indian Ocean to Box 666 in Twisp in a week. Did the letter land in Cairo? I bet it went to Paris.

I covered the miles to home seated at 50 mph, put more wood on the fire, carried water to the barn, collected eggs, spoke to my cats about this and that and spoke to my father in Washington, D.C.

Living with so much I don't understand, I find contrasts becoming old hat. I'm getting edgy that it's going to take more and more to shift my sense of wonder into high gear.

(March 1986)

Chapter IV

Helicopters, Gravestones and Fish

The first time Charley Schmidt came to the Methow Valley was in 1914 on a fishing trip. He drove an Overland car. He and a few of his family piled in at sunrise at Waterville and finally arrived in Winthrop after an arduous journey. They had gotten stuck in the sand several times and had to back up every hill so the gas could flow into the carburetor. They spent the night in Winthrop, and the next morning Charley discovered that he needed a fishing license that could be gotten only in Conconully.

So he and friend got back into the car, backed up all the hills, got stuck in the sand, and made it to Conconully by noon. The official had no licenses. However, he wrote a note saying that Charley was authorized to fish the waters of Okanogan County. Charley paid his 50 cents, got back into the car, got stuck in the sand, backed up all the hills, and got back to Winthrop that night.

Luckily, the fishing was great.

"The water was just lousy with fish," Charley beamed.

Persistence. That's what these following pieces are all about. They're also about the personal touch that still survives in this small community.

One day, I was peering through the locked glass door of the empty Hiway Radio shop, wondering where Charley Breslin was. Across the street, Dan Johnson, minding my business, stood beside his barber pole munching an apple.

"Charley'll be back in about twenty minutes," he called over to me. "He's gone home for lunch."

"Oh?" I said, "and what's he having for lunch?"

"Nothing very good," Dan replied. "His wife's away."

The Priscilla Club

"You know the best thing about this club?" pressed Sylvia Christianson, 82. "We don't have to do a darn thing but visit."

"Absolutely," agreed Eadie Lull, a third-generation member. "We're a do-nothing club. I'd say the most remarkable thing about it and its longevity is that it's never had any goals or high ideals, and has survived on friendship alone."

The club so fondly described is the Twisp Priscilla Club, founded in 1909, one of the oldest continuing organizations in Okanogan County.

For 77 years the 22 ladies of the club have convened on first and third Wednesdays at each one's house in turn. The membership has remained fairly constant over the decades so that each woman entertains once a year.

At the gatherings there is never any doubt that the conversation will be lively, the dessert delicious, the table setting impeccable, and the company, of course, flawless.

Only once, during World War II, the Priscillas broke out of their constitutionally condoned idleness to pool their sewing talents to create a red and white satin war service flag which waved in Methow Valley breezes for a time.

Except for a few missing notebooks from the '30s and the '40s, minutes taken at the get-togethers have been preserved.

They are hardly documents of tremendous import. "In all the records, not one negative adjective was ever used to describe the food served," said Eadie, who is in the process of compiling a club history. "I can't tell you how many times I read the words, 'delicious dessert,' " she chuckled.

A quote from the May 12, 1915, minutes reads, "Luncheon was served, interspersed with pleasant chat." Seventy years later it might read the same.

Even their treasury reflects the members' priority to socialize rather than to raise funds for any cause. Dues are one dollar a year, and 25 cent fines are imposed on forgetful ladies who fail to call a hostess about missing a meeting. A record low balance of 20 cents was recorded in September 1923, after a going-away present was bought for a member.

From the minutes of December 29, 1926, it was learned, "The question of entertaining our husbands was brought before the club, but received indifferent attention and was dropped."

Originally called "The Shakespeare Club" in 1910, that intimidating name was changed to "The Embroidery Club," perhaps giving a more accurate picture of how the women spent their time while chatting.

Not long afterwards the group re-titled itself the Priscilla Club, which held, probably because it pretended no lofty purpose.

Since no one knows for sure, one has to suppose that Marjorie Delvendahl organized the club to make a woman's pioneer life in the Methow Valley a little more palatable. Social life was undeniably and tediously limited. No telephones connected friends, no televisions offered false company, and horse and buggies were harder to start than Chevrolets.

The member whose turn it is to entertain abolishes dust and unshrouds her best china. Everyone arrives dressed to the nines, lending the gatherings a definite air of formality, a holdover from a more proper era.

If they have a reputation as gossips, it's a false one, they say. An unwritten rule stops all negative talk. Instead, they bring pictures to show, or talk about books they've read, or activities and trips they've taken since the last meeting.

Get-well cards are signed and sent to sick members, and if one has died, they discuss who might take her place. One must be invited.

The Twisp Priscilla Club holds a prominent place in these women's lives, otherwise they wouldn't have answered the invitation to join.

Says Cecile Nickell, the club's oldest member at 94, "They're all very special people. It gives me a chance to visit with them."

Eadie is the youngest Priscilla. "I treasure these people I've known so long. They knew my family. For me, they're a link to what was good in my childhood."

(November 1986)

Behind the Chutes

Bull riders are a special breed. When the chute gate opens, thousands of pounds of horned fury explode into the arena. The man whose leather-sheathed hand is practically riveted to the rope around the bull's girth has a couple of options: he'll either walk away from the experience or he'll be carried away from it.

To watch these men-boys lower themselves down onto the wide backs of beasts never broken to ride is to watch determination epitomized.

A half an hour before they climb over the boards to let themselves down onto the bulls, they pace the enclosure behind the chutes where all the saddles and tack and gear of rodeos is littered. They psyche themselves up. They get angry. They don't see a thing beyond their eyeballs. They swear. They bash the air with their fists. They think bad thoughts. They kick out at unknown forces beyond normal vision.

The rage they create must match the rage of the bull, otherwise the contest will be uneven. Behind the chutes, the air is electric with hate.

Rodeo fans sipping beer on their tailgates only see the tail end of the battle.

(May 1985)

Boy Born in Church Basement

In the basement of the Assembly of God church in Twisp last Wednesday night, Dale Ingersoll gave birth to her sixth child in the company of 14 children and 11 adults.

Dale and Lewis Ingersoll and their five children have lived in the church's basement this winter and had planned to have a home delivery. The fact that there were so many people around during the birth "just sort of happened," but it was fine with her and she claims the experience was "really fun."

The nine pound baby boy has not yet been named because, says Dale, "I was thinking girl so hard, and her name was going to be Faith. We call him Sweetie Pie and things to that effect now. We'll just wait and see what his personality is like before naming him."

The baby is the Ingersoll's fifth boy.

"Someday we're going to have a large family," jokes Lewis seriously. It's common knowledge the Ingersolls want lots of children around and, who knows, they may really be only half way through producing them.

Aside from two children she had in a hospital, the rest have been home deliveries, and Lewis has been present at all of them. This is the first time the rest of the family was present.

"I didn't think there'd be any surprises," says Dale, "and there weren't any. With your sixth it doesn't get heavy until the end. At one point I looked up and saw rows and rows of faces."

"There was a sex education class that night," smiles Lewis.

"I was glad those people were there to see it," continues Dale, "especially those who had never had any children of their own. The kids could see that it's not a scary thing, that you don't have to scream and yell, that you don't have to work too hard. It's not hard if you're not afraid of the unknown."

One adult present at the birth commented, "She made it look so easy."

Dale had been up all day even though she had begun to feel labor pains. At 7:30 that evening she lay down, began having hard cramps at 8, and delivered the child into her husband's hands at 8:15.

The family has lived in the valley for two years and came from the piney woods of east Texas. Lewis works at the sawmill. They are a strong (and growing) part of the Christian community in the Methow Valley.

(March 1980)

The Town of Methow

Twenty-two miles south of Twisp, after innumerable kinks in the river and swoops in the road, the unincorporated town of Methow, population guessed at about 65, sits pretty on another curve in both river and road.

Most visitors to, and residents of, the rest of the Methow Valley tend to take the town at 55 mph and two breaths worth of time, but the folks of Methow think the world of their hometown, or else they wouldn't be there.

Two swinging bridges (one in perfect condition) span the Methow River at either end of town and reach for the apple orchards on the other side. Wood-framed houses jumble along with mobile homes down the street that doglegs off the highway, past the old hotel, abandoned now, where Gussie Bolinger used to shoot chickens with her .22 when guests dropped in. That street meanders down toward the river where the old schoolhouse has been turned into the Community Club where residents vote, meet for Grange, and hold receptions for sons' or daughters' weddings.

The fourth-class post office squats on the highway, which bisects the town. Tiny and shingled, it accommodates more than 100 mailboxes, many for people living up French, McFarland, Squaw, and Black creeks.

The fire engine just fits the building next door.

Twenty-nine people attended church last Sunday, according to the chart on the wall, which also announced the numbers of the hymns sung and that $8.62 had been collected.

John Ball, a Methow resident for 75 years, praises Larry Trim, the church's pastor for the past score of years. "He doesn't care about your denomination, he just goes out and helps people," a resident reported. "I don't know what they would do without him here."

Across the street, Mike's Market has been boarded up for several years and doesn't have the air of wanting to be opened up again too soon, but next door to it, at King's Lunch, business thrives.

Functioning as Methow's community center, the cafe-tavern-pool hall-message and package receiving depot has been run by John and Punky

Wingard since May.

"I was fed up with working for someone else," said John, former employee of Alaska Airlines. "I cried for two days when I came here, this place and the people were so beautiful. I get emotional when things are pretty and nice," he clarified.

"I once heard someone describe the people who live here as earthbound," he said. "In the city, there are so many flakes. People here have common sense. The weather's harsh and common sense is the only thing'll pull you through, I guess."

Dick Seiler, newly arrived on French Creek after having been laid off at Boeing, couldn't stop saying good things about Methow.

"You ask someone if you can fish on their property, they walk you down to their best hole, and bait your hook for you." He laughed with the wonder of it.

"I had only been here for an hour," he recounted about his arrival in December, "no one knew who I was and yet I was totally accepted. There's not a person in town who wouldn't bend over backwards for you. It's that earthbound stuff again."

John Ball's attitude toward newcomers is, in fact, down-to-earth. "They move in and they're just there, that's all. You get acquainted with them; it's all right," he allowed. Outside King's Lunch two gas pumps wore old signs: "Out of gas."

"I'll get some gas in them this summer." John said. "Maybe."

John's sense of urban competitiveness has faded since he's moved to the town at the bend in the road.

(January 1982)

Army Helicopters Park in Thistle

The U.S. Army's newest advance attack helicopters, with weaponry capable of making "the best Soviet tank look like a piece of Swiss cheese," are presently parked at Twisp's airport where young pilots are receiving tactical training in low-level flying and high pinnacle approaches in the surrounding mountains.

About 35 soldiers of the Alpha Company #268 Attack Helicopter Battalion from Fort Lewis' 9th Infantry are camped in the barnaby thistle until the end of the week. This is about the fifth year that the Army has conducted mountain maneuvers while based in the Methow Valley.

This year new equipment is being tested. Three Cobra Tow Gunships, streamlined, silent and deadly, will be handled by men trying to learn the craft's capabilities.

"I pity the Soviets, I really do," asserted Staff Sergeant Portz while explaining some of the features. "As long as they don't go nuclear," he added. "If they go nuclear nobody's going to win."

He went on to say that the Soviets have similar aircraft, "but the only difference is here," he emphasized, slapping the pilot's seat, "the man who sits here. We'd rather put the equipment to the ultimate test and save the man. They think the other way around."

The helicopter alone, minus its missiles, rockets and cannon ammunition, is worth $3.2 million. "They're lethal," said Portz, "and designed to deliver first-round kill. By the way, we're more than happy to show off our equipment to anyone who wants to drop by. These are YOUR helicopters."

The local fire departments and sawmill have challenged the visiting boys to a few friendly baseball games Thursday night at 7. The public is invited.

(August 1981)

Dog Clips

"My favorite type of dog is the non-nervous dog," smiled Sharon Ziesseniss wryly as she clipped the ears of a well-behaved apricot poodle named Bingo.

Sharon, who works for the Dan DeWeerts in several other capacities at their veterinary clinic south of Twisp, began learning the canine clipping business in June "because I had a dog and didn't want to take it all the way to Omak all the time."

"The most difficult dogs to clip are scared dogs," explained Candy DeWeert. "There are almost no mean dogs here in the valley. We end up tranquilizing only about one in a hundred.

"We're not show clippers," she went on. "We don't do fancy cutting on poodles. Basically, we do what we like to call the 'summer cut.' Nice and neat and short. It's for people who don't want their dogs' hair full of grass, burrs and weeds. We get some pretty dirty dogs and we end up doing cleanup jobs."

When asked directly, Candy admitted, "You never have one hundred percent satisfied customers. What we strive for is not to make the same mistake twice, so the people won't go up town and say bad things."

At least Bingo looked entirely satisfied. She sat tranquil and slightly bored while Sharon clipped between her toes. Two other dogs, already groomed, waited patiently for their owners to return.

(November 1983)

Beat the Blues: Pound on Dough

Feeling out of synch? Cast off, cast out, cast down?

Pay $50 an hour no longer. A lifting of your spirit is no farther away than your very own kitchen.

For untold numbers of pioneer women – who would have shrunk from shrinks even if shrinks had been slinking around – this therapy worked.

The secret? Baking bread.

According to Lillian Lemaster of Twisp, her mother was able every time to bake herself into a better frame of mind. Friends always knew that Edna Estes had just set herself to rights when they smelt the aroma of fresh cinnamon rolls emanating from her house.

"It's the dough," elucidated Lillian. "Just pounding the heck out of it." Lillian uses the same method to put her own life back into perspective.

The other day she was slightly out of sorts because her oven was on the fritz. Having to resort to cutting quilt blocks, she found that the cold slithering of steel scissors across thin cloth just didn't do the trick. She'd needed to plunge her fists into great gobs of warm yeasty pliable batterable malleable stretchy bouncy dough. She'd longed to throw her weight into billows of the unresisting stuff.

She'd also missed the finale.

When the session is over, when you've flung yourself on the davenport to feel well-being flow back into your addled soul, you know that in a very short time you'll be sinking your teeth into thick hot freshly buttered slabs of honest-to-god Goodness itself.

Shrinks, on the other hand, just want the dough. Raw.

(February 1987)

The Old Cemetery

Mrs. Della E. Mack's gravestone, obscured by barnaby thistle and dry grasses, leans propped up against a rock at the east end of Belsby's field. Time and again the marker has been knocked over by grazing cattle and time and again it has been righted.

On it is this inscription:

"All my heart is buried with you,
All my thoughts go onward with you.
Come not back again to labor,
Come not back again to suffer.
Soon my task will be completed,
Soon your footsteps I shall follow."

In 1901 Mrs. Mack's remains were sunk into the soil of Winthrop's original cemetery, just behind the middle school and over the barbed wire fence of the Belsby ranch.

Clarence Heckendorn remembered her. "Oh, yes, she drowned in the Methow. They picked her up off the riffle above where the bridge is. Her husband was a blacksmith. I was just a little boy at the time. I believe it was suicide."

During the few years that site was used as a burying ground, bodies and mourners had to either ford the river or go all the way around to Twisp and up the other side of the river to reach the cemetery. The first occupant of the final resting place was Ella Cromwell, 24, the first cancer victim in the Methow. Her headboard can be viewed at Winthrop's Shafer Museum.

In 1903, when Heckendorn's father sold some hilltop ground to the town for $50 for what became Sullivan's Cemetery, many of the original corpses were exhumed and reburied up on the flat. A few, like 38-year-old Mrs. Della Mack, remained where she was, since no relatives came forward to give permission.

For many years, at least through the '40s, a white picket fence surrounded the few remaining graves on what was then called the Spring Creek Dairy. Now even that fence is gone, and it's been many decades since Mr. A. H. Mack followed Della's footsteps, as he promised he would.

(July 1981)

The Force Behind School Lunches

Lois Chavey

Hot school lunches don't just appear, as if by magic: Abracadabra! Four hundred and fifty-six hamburgers! Gallons of salad! Acres of jello! Basins of gravy! Baked potatoes by the hundred-weight! There are figures, but only a few, behind those facts. They add up to two cooks and two helpers. How often do the students and teachers consider where it all comes from? Students, preoccupied with algebraic equations, verbs and myths; teachers, mulling over presentation, absenteeism, and interest levels, all explode at noontime out of classrooms and into corridors and head directly to lunch, where it's all spread out ready for the hungry hordes.

Every school day Lois Chavey, Number One cook, and Ruth Webb, Number Two, meet at the bus barn in Twisp at 5:40 a.m. for the five minute drive to Allen Elementary in the school food van. Long before cockcrow these two women are commencing the process that will have lunch for around 430 students and teachers ready for transporting to the three schools at 10:40. At 8 a.m. Marge Nilles and Sue Sabin join the chefs to help wash, chop, shred, and mix whatever needs to be washed, chopped, shredded or mixed.

Last week was National Hot Lunch Week. To pay homage to the technological world on Tuesday, school cooks all over the USA prepared Power Source Burgers, Printout Potatoes, Vegetable Chips, Apple Bytes and Basic Milk.

Lois and Ruth were no exception. While Lois steam-heated 456 hamburgers, Ruth mixed dough with aid from the Hobart mixer to make the buns. (All hamburger and hot dog buns are homemade in the Methow Valley School District.) Huge trays piled high with tater tots got slipped into the ovens, hundreds of carrots were sliced, lengthwise, a new sauce was concocted (Marge: "How much of this mayonnaise goes in here?" Lois: "Oh, some. I never measure it.") and applesauce from local apples, made the day before, was poured into traveling containers.

In storage rooms nightmare-sized shakers loom from shelves: six pound cans of paprika, two-and-a-half pounds of basil, three pounds of cinnamon. Cases of peanut butter don't last long.

The kitchen doesn't seem big enough to prepare a many-itemed meal for so many people but somehow the four women are able to maneuver themselves around with oversized trays, sliding them into tray holders, warming boxes, slots and drawers. They juggle 10-gallon soup pots, gargantuan bowls and buckets of fresh vegetables so that the entire meal is warmed in two ovens or on one stove, or gets cooled in walk-in coolers so that, in less than five hours, lunch is ready.

Stringent national guidelines dictate the correct balance of protein and vitamins for each meal, and government commodities such as butter, cheese, powdered milk and flour must be worked into the program, the cooks said. Despite the rules, the chefs take pride in trying to prepare menus the kids like.

"Quite a bit of psychology goes into the preparation," Lois said. "If we're serving something they don't particularly like, we'll throw in something special, like chocolate milk. Celery sticks: they don't like them," she said with a knowing smile. "We've finally found a way the kids'll eat chicken: dipped in buttermilk and dried bread crumbs and oven-baked."

Local produce like Evans' potatoes and Schulz's apples are used when possible. The most difficult meals they make, they all agree, are the ones when they bake either maple bars or cinnamon rolls.

Whatever plate waste cannot be incorporated into another meal is given to janitor Joe Setting for his chickens.

At 10:30 a.m., if their deadline has been successfully met, the four can sit down for the first time. In 10 minutes, however, they are up again, loading the containers, buckets and heating boxes into the van for the trip to the high school and junior high, where Sue and Ruth serve.

After the meal has been consumed in the three schools, they wash up and put the trays back in the van and return to the grade school for the final neatening up. At 2 p.m. their work is done. Then they can all go home and clean their houses and get dinner ready.

(October 1983)

Hunters up Elbow Coulee

Every hunting season, the valley becomes stippled with temporary camps made up of one or more vehicles more or less equipped to feel like miniature homes. In the woods, up draws, down dirt roads, beside creeks, vehicles circle like covered wagons. These camps appear for a weekend or a week, then disappear when the hunters' time is up.

Last week this reporter snooped around one camp, being curious about who the people were and what they'd been doing.

Seven hunters, two wives, two children and four dogs was the sudden population of this particular camp up Elbow Coulee. Trailers named Tioga, Prowler and Companion formed a circle around a rock-rimmed campfire that "had been going for a week."

The folks were in the process of dismantling the campsite. Some were going home to Kent, Federal Way, Auburn, Seattle; the three "bachelors" were off to the Republic area to hunt grouse and bear. One of them was a King County detective, another a football player for the Tampa Bay Bears. The kids pursued salamanders up until the last minute.

In one week they'd bagged one two-point and one grouse, yet they still considered their stay "successful."

"We came here to have a good time," said one. "Besides, if you get a deer, you have to quit hunting."

Bill Browning said he'd been camping in Elbow Coulee every hunting season for 22 years, had come as a child with his father. Now his friends fill the familiar campsite.

"I love it over here," he said. "We're all sentimental about the coulee. We've always gone away with at least one deer every year."

Among the seven hunters, eight or 10 bucks had been sighted but they'd fired only one shot.

Pat Henne, one of the two wives, felt she had been brought along "to do the cooking for the family" (the salamander catchers were hers) "and keep my husband's feet warm." But she'd had a great time, she added.

They had brought along generators for lights ("we're not exactly roughing it too bad") and would sit around the fire at night "telling lies and dirty stories." The men would get up at 5, pile into the biggest of the trailers for coffee and rolls, lay out their moves for the day, and before rolling out of camp, "make the fire for the girls."

The next day that hunters' camp up the coulee was a blank spot by the hills, a smudge of char where the fire'd burned, a few tire tracks, and three relieved salamanders.

(October 1983)

Richard's Hands

When I first met Richard Wrangle my eyes were immediately drawn to his hands. As closely as possible, they resembled my mother's. I liked Richard on sight because of them. He too downplayed his pain.

My mother's hands were like wounded birds she held gently in her lap, one lying lightly over the other. Around one wrist she always tied a jaunty silk scarf.

Her hands were like no other hands I knew. They had valleys and hills where other mothers' hands had only plains. They broadened and swelled, and could, I suppose, have been thought grotesque. But I thought them lovely, all hers, and I'm now sorry I never photographed them.

Feeling that her pain was a boring subject, she never complained about the rheumatoid arthritis that had crippled her. It was simply her pain and she wouldn't inflict it on others.

Having never been a particularly manual person, her dexterity was largely relegated to bringing glasses to her lips or forks to her mouth, though even those basics cost her.

After I met Richard's hands, I was introduced to his furniture.

Something didn't jibe. How could there possibly be any connection between those hands and these stunning pieces of art? I had seldom seen furniture so sensual, so curved and inviting. He made utilitarian objects intimate; each piece sang of its own existence.

In the 30 years that Richard has had rheumatoid arthritis, he has turned hundreds of pounds of rough slab wood and tree butts into exquisite desks and stools and tables and lamps.

How could he do it? More specifically, why isn't pain reflected in his work?

A thoughtful man, Richard has considered these questions for years.

"I don't reflect the pain because I have such a sense of perfectionism," he began. "This trait has allowed me to work my way through the pain without problems. I feel intensely the beauty of this planet. I detest grotesque art which introduces people to the violence and ugliness humans inflict on each other. It may be self-deception, but I have struggled to eliminate all ugliness from my work, even though I know it exists."

Some experts in the disease contend that the progressively crippling malady, which deteriorates the body's joints, is caused or aggravated by the victim's nature, that it strikes those who suppress their natural tendencies, or who are otherwise in conflict with themselves.

"I have a tension in me which lets me feel design," Richard went on, "and at the same time I am extremely critical of the craft. Without that tension, I don't believe I could have done the work I've done, but it also could be the reason for my arthritis. To not be able to create would be hell for me. If that is why my arthritis exists, then I accept that. I wouldn't take the trade off."

Besides their own creative work, Richard and his wife Cheryl tirelessly encourage local artists and help bring outside works into the Methow Valley through art groups of which they are charter members.

(September 1988)

Sheep Come Off the Range

Like tumbleweeds on a roll, sheep by the hundreds poured down steep slopes into Rattlesnake Campground corrals, their hoofs casting dust high into the fall-crisp air.

Two black collies attuned to Spanish commands dogged stragglers' heels while Enrique Cajachagua followed surefooted at the herd's rear.

Their summer in the wilds was over. Trucks waited in the upper Methow Valley to carry them home.

This band of sheep, 2,400 strong, was just one of Simon Martinez' many bands set free of fences to forage on summer ranges around the central part of the state.

These particular ewes and their lambs, shepherded by two Peruvians and their dogs, had just spent three-and-a-half months on the Sawtooth and Pasayten wilderness ranges.

In the past, vast numbers of sheep grazed on the Okanogan National Forest. But more stringent conservation regulations imposed by the Forest Service pared down the amount so drastically that only Martinez may run his flocks in that terrain. In fact, he's been the only permit holder since the mid-1970s.

Range conservationists frequently patrol sheep driveways to make sure that feed is abundant and that the soil is firm enough to accommodate the ungulates.

Predators add another dimension to the story. There are always losses. This year about a hundred head were killed by coyotes in the Sawtooth.

It was easier to control coyotes when chemical means were allowed, Martinez said, but chemicals were outlawed. Now, a propane-powered "cannon," placed a discreet distance from the shepherds' camp, blasts off every 15 minutes. The sound is calculated to dissuade coyotes from even thinking about having lamb for a midnight snack.

Enrique Cajachagua has herded Martinez' sheep in the surrounding hills for about 10 years. This year his assistant, Pedro, newly arrived from

Peru, helped him keep watch.

On a typical day, the men and their two dogs would rise with the light and drive the sheep out in a new direction. During the day they'd circle the moving congregation of ewes and lambs, "wearing out a good pair of boots every 15 days," joked Enrique. As daylight faded, the sheep would meander back to be near the camp, sensing that the men's presence meant security.

Depending on the amount of forage, Enrique and Pedro would move their campsite every two or three days. Since little rain fell this summer, breaking camp was a more frequent operation than in other years.

The day the sheep cascaded into Rattlesnake corrals, Pedro looked relieved to be back among people. Enrique, on the other hand, kept slipping back into the woods, keeping an eye on the band, reluctant to leave the wilderness behind.

(September 1986)

Winthrop for Lease

What's wrong with this picture?

Here's a spiffed up Western-type town, humming with tourists, with a complex of shops off to one side but most attractively situated, bordered with wood decking and perched above the confluence of the Methow and Chewuch rivers.

Look closer. Scotch taped to all five glass doors of the main Winthrop Marketplace building are "For Lease" signs. And if you cup your eyes to the windows, you can see that it's all empty, scooped clean of any enterprise.

Last summer specialty chocolates, barbecued salmon, outdoor gear, good cheeses and local artwork could be bought here. Today, the few tourists lured the hundred yards past the supposed end of the boardwalk find themselves in a well-manicured but strangely desolate outdoor mall.

Someone's dream, looks like, has not come true.

Three years ago, Methow Valley realtor Doug Sylvester got swept up in the positive mood of the valley, studied the situation's potential, and set out to carefully plan what he considered to be a retailer's paradise.

Nowadays he sits in his North Cascade Realty office and admits he's frustrated.

"In the past two-and-a-half years," he said, searching for culprits, "the amount of leased retail space in Winthrop has increased somewhere between two and three times. A small town like this can only absorb so much. The name of the game is number of people, and the valley's population simply isn't great enough to accommodate this much retail space. Also, our complex is just that bit more remote (a few hundred feet) from the core of town, so perhaps it's not ideal."

The erzatz Western theme town is three blocks long. Its nearest neighboring town to the west that has a tavern is 89 miles away, with the spine of the North Cascade Mountains intervening.

"Obviously," Sylvester concluded wistfully, "it's risky business being involved in development. I've come to the conclusion that in my next life I'm steering clear of this sort of thing. I want to live the simple life."

(July 1987)

Loki's Obit

Loki's gone.

Loki, dog of Twisp, will no longer be making his appointed rounds of town. Nor will he stand by the school children waiting for their morning bus. The mini-mart and senior citizen center can put their dog dishes away forever, because Loki won't be coming around to visit and politely eat. Kenny the bread man won't need to break open new packages of Hostess Twinkies anymore, nor will the Evergreen grocery or Hank's supermarket clerks have to look for scraps to feed that personable canine gentleman who nearly daily, for 10 years, plied his varied route throughout Twisp.

"It's almost as if he were a symbol, not a dog," said Cindy Button, one of Loki's "real" parents, and she's right. He was a friend, companion, familiar landmark, a fixture, the town greeter.

Loki possessed a practiced sense of self-preservation. He looked both ways before crossing the road, and sometimes, when he was tired and achy, he'd walk the half mile up to the clinic and bum a ride home with Dr. Henry. "He always thought that was shorter than going directly home," laughed Cindy, but his legs knew what his legs knew. And he got there just about the time either Cindy or the doctor closed up shop.

When he'd get home he'd eat his meal just as if he hadn't had 20 handouts during the day. One might have to suspect he did it just to be nice to his real family.

There were days, Cindy said, when he just stayed in bed all day. Sometimes the company of man must have seemed, even for a dog of Loki's nature, too much to bear.

Rumors have it Loki didn't bother females of his species. In fact, Cindy has a friend who told her about when her two bitches came in heat, Loki dropped by to sit there and keep all the other dogs away, "sort of preserving the girls' purity."

On November 5, Loki was found dead near the Forest Service compound in Twisp, victim of poisoning. No one knows what it was he ate or how he came by it, but the hard, cold fact remains: none of us will see Loki again plodding with doggy determination up and down the streets of Twisp.

(November 1985)

Cattle Drives: A Dying Art?

As of last week's snow storm the last of the range cattle that had summered as far away as the Canadian border were home for the winter, driven down valley roads to within bellowing distance of a hay stack.

While cattle drives are not uncommon in the Methow Valley, how much longer can they remain a part of the local scene? How long before what is expedient becomes a nuisance? In time, the pace of a cow's ambling might conflict with the pace of today's sped-up lifestyle.

"During real cold weather or a storm, cows don't like to move very fast," said Millie Bagwell as she led her herd of 80 down the east side road.

"Unless they find a hole in the fence," retorted son George Moore.

Some local ranchers have had to resort to the more arduous and expensive method of trucking. The Frank Thurlows used to drive their large herds from Carlton to Beaver Creek but haven't done so since the opening of the North Cascades Highway in 1972 because of increased car traffic. It now takes them two weeks to load and truck the animals to their rangeland, a far more lengthy operation.

"Some people become very impatient" when they have to drive their cars the speed a cow walks, explained Lucille Thurlow.

Wayne Frost, who drives Mack Lloyd's cattle to the Rendezvous hills from Pearrygin Lake, encounters particularly tricky situations because his route takes him directly through downtown Winthrop.

Tourists and locals wielding cameras startle the animals, the bridge over the Chewuch spooks them, Pool Hall Hill entices them to make a break for it. Unfenced gardens become cow paths, and town intersections become frantic scenes of confusion.

"If you don't know how to grin and apologize, you're better off leaving those cattle at home," Wayne advised. "I can swear by cattle in the hills, but look out when they're in town. Cows aren't dumb, they just have a limited capacity."

He explained that if a cow gets separated from her calf, she will turn around and go straight back to where it last suckled. The calf will do the same. Allowing cows and calves to pair up is an important part of the herding skill. The last thing any rider wants is 300 traumatized mothers and children bawling for each other and breaking for home.

As traffic in the valley becomes heavier, will drivers have to resort to trucking their animals? Cattle drives, like lookout towers and house parties and nice telephone operators might, in the near future, just become another piece of our history.

In the meantime, the next time you careen around a corner and come face to face with a sea of cattle, recognize the sensitive task of those riding herd. They have enough to do second-guessing a bunch of cows.

(December 1984)

William Charley Talks on the Methow Language

William Charley

"I'm not only going to teach my students to talk the Methow language, at the end of twenty weeks they are going to act like I do and think like I do. They will be a group that will have power; they will see what has to be done and they will do it. They will be a breed of people nobody can hurt."

So spoke William Charley last week at a gathering in Twisp.

William Charley is an Indian of the Methow band, one of the 11 bands within the Colville Confederated Tribes.

"My generation is the very last to speak the Methow language," he said. "Our role is to pass our knowledge to the next generation."

In his Omak home he has started a school to teach the language. A few more than a thousand words constitute the Methow vocabulary.

William grew up speaking Methow and four other Indian languages, learning English when he was nine or 10 years old.

"I'm also trying to bring back the storytelling heritage," he went on.

"We used to stay for three or four days with a family just telling the stories and legends of our people. We had a lot of time in the old days. We traveled by horseback so we knew what was going on all the time. People today are always looking at their watches. We used to have all the time in the world."

He would like to hold storytelling sessions in elders' homes and speak in the Methow language. The best storytelling time is in the winter. He would ask the elders if he could record them in order to preserve the legends and language for future generations.

"That would be beautiful," he smiled.

(November 1981)

Women at the Sawmill

Up until this spring Twisp's sawmill was a man's domain. Swirled in sawdust in the half-light of the screeching and pounding multi-leveled main mill building, hard-hatted men went about their labors swearing when they felt like it and moving with assurance through the noise of the powerful machines.

In May a new element was added to the workforce: women. If the men resented this sudden intrusion into their fortress, they haven't shown it, according to the four women who work there now among 94 men on the three shifts.

"I expected resentment," said d'Arlene Hadfield, weigher and scaler.

Diane Hope said she felt embarrassed to have to ring the bell for help so often in her first days, but found that the men were so helpful and friendly that she gained confidence in herself. She now looks as assured around the machinery as any of the men.

"I used to be your typical housewife," she said. "I was very caught up in that world, but I feel that outside the home you express more of your own personality."

Nevertheless, money is the main motive for taking a job at the mill. At a beginning wage of $6.92 an hour, few women can make more than that in this area.

"I'm just trying to make a living like any other guy," stated Peggy Elkins, who has worked on cleanup in the dry kiln area of the grounds for the past month.

At the mill for two-and-a-half months, Diane was already filling in for someone at a job that entails making sure the scrap lumber moves smoothly along the shaking conveyor trough into a revolving chipper.

Since it was impossible to talk alongside the shattering noise, she and I stood quietly together while we waited for her replacement. Finally she turned to me and screamed into my ear, "It sure is hard for two women to be standing together and not be able to say anything!"

Later, after we'd made our way to the break room, I asked one man what he felt about having women at the mill.

"It don't bug me any," he allowed.

Ian Irvine, mill manager, is more complimentary about the women he has hired. "We've been dang lucky in the women we've gotten," he said.

D'Arlene and Diane both expressed the fact that they felt happier about themselves since they began their jobs. Diane added even more weight to her statement by adding, "I'd like to hang in here for twenty years."

(September 1978)

Fishing Stories from Eileen Horey

Once upon a time an orphan boy ran away from his foster home to join the Barnum and Bailey circus. No acrobat or tamer of lions, he pitched tent and tightened the ropes to hold it up.

That boy eventually made his way across a raw United States and ended up teaching several generations of kids music in a dead-end town named Winthrop. During his lifetime the town never did amount to much.

His name was Jerry Sullivan and he met a pretty, shy girl named Goldie. They honeymooned beside Eightmile Creek and some lyrical mapmaker named the spot after the pair's wedding holiday.

They named a daughter Eileen and he taught her to fish because early on she seemed to show a preference for being outside, and she learned fast.

Her parents are now at rest in Sullivan (no relation) Cemetery on the hill over Winthrop, and Eileen is back home after a long absence.

Her eyes still glow when she talks about fishing long ago in the Methow.

"When I was seven or eight," she began, "I went down to the river just this side of Winthrop and saw an enormous salmon. It was just resting near some rocks. I ran and told my father, who came back with me reluctantly because he was having luck of his own farther downriver. But when he saw it he was surprised to see how big it was. He stood there a minute, calculating, then he lunged in and grabbed that thing by the tail and heaved it so far up the bank it reached the road. I ran up there and threw myself on it, wrestling around with it until we both got tired. Then I took hold of it by the tail and flipped it over my shoulder and walked home with it, along the road. Its head knocked against the back of my legs. People honked their horns at us as they passed.

"Another time when I was very young my father took me up to Thirtymile to watch the Indians fish for salmon. You could smell their camp long before you got to it. They split and dried their fish, leaving the guts lying around. Flies, dogs, and kids were everywhere.

"Here's how the Indians caught their fish. They'd build a screen of willow branches across the stream, leaving one hole in it. A salmon swimming upstream would encounter the screen, nose around until it found the hole, swim through and find itself trapped in a willow basket.

"An Indian, still as a statue, would be waiting. When a fish found itself in the basket the Indian would lance it with a spear and flip it to shore, where a woman would clean it."

Eileen has not forgotten the techniques of fishing her father taught her. "I learned serious fishing from the start. I never spoke, never made unnecessary noise. The north fork streams were our favorites."

Needless to say, fishing season is Eileen's favorite season.

(April 1985)

Christian Community's Second Generation

The Christian community began with a casual comment tossed into the air during dinner with friends in California.

"Maybe," one of them said, "we can do something for the Lord with that piece of land."

The land was 140 acres of hillside and valley bottom, located six miles from Twisp up Poorman Creek.

Less than a year later, five families, all determined to flesh out the ideas that had shaken them loose from their secure routines in southern California, loaded up their belongings and young children, and headed north to the Methow Valley.

The Christian community, which they agreed to call Second Mile Ranch, was inaugurated.

Fifteen years later, eight homes grace the sprawling property. Houses and land are owned by the six extended families in common, meaning if anyone leaves they may not sell their house. Because of this, most of the adults hope their children will eventually return to live on the ranch.

Of the 20 or more members of the second generation, toddlers when they were first brought to this mountain valley, many are now teenagers in the local high school. Others are in college around the state. The oldest is 22.

They're now at an age to wonder how Second Mile will figure into the remainder of their lives.

Fifteen years ago their parents were idealists, excited to exchange a materialistic way of life for one more attuned to Christian principles. They believed they could live with little and hoped their children would ultimately be fired by the same enthusiasm.

Over the ensuing years, the goals for the ranch changed radically. Communal projects, from growing sunflowers to running a sawmill, eventually dissolved or became individual pursuits.

Today, the families are held together by the Tenancy in Common

Agreement and a formal statement of purpose: "To show forth through our lives the existence of a personal God." They gather for Tuesday night potlucks, hold regular business meetings and throw a Christmas party. Otherwise, they live their own lives.

According to Wayne Mendro, one of the ranch's charter members, "The ideals of the ranch have changed to such a degree that I see it more as a neighborhood than a Christian entity."

So the question remains: will the second generation, armed with Christian values, opt to remain on the ranch, thereby refusing to adopt mainstream America's secular fascination with material goods and security?

Not likely, seems to be the general consensus.

Jim Floyd, a freshman at Western Washington University, said that although he is glad he grew up on the ranch because the people there are the best he's met in his life, he would return "but only after I've completed what I've wanted to do in life."

His sister Pam, a senior at Western Washington, echoed the same sentiment.

"I want to go back to live on the ranch, but not too soon. Probably when I'm retired."

Annie Schmekel, a sophomore at Liberty Bell High School, explained, "I'd like to move to a city in California, because I like meeting new people. I like the idea of a different environment than here. But I'll come back here all the time. Maybe I'll bring my kids up in the city, then return."

Said Sara Shaffer, sixth grade, "I don't really like the city; it's just weird being there. But there's not very much going on here either."

Her brother, Michael, added, "There's not enough excitement here."

Aaron Westlund, 15, said, "It's more foreign in a city. Here, you go out the back door and go skiing instead of seeing crowds of unknown faces. But I want to get out of the Methow Valley after high school and see what the rest of the world's like. I'll eventually live here, though."

Both Mendro offspring believe it would be unfair to the people they marry to return to the ranch, where their mates would feel left out of a communally shared past.

Ben, 22, graduate of Seattle Pacific University, called the ranch a "womb" and thinks that returning to live there is "a pretty unrealistic idea. I've gotten pretty urbane," he admitted. "I think I'd go crazy. There's so much to do in Seattle. My romantic notions about the place got shattered as I got older. Besides, I'm excited about making my own life."

Michelle Shaffer, a senior at Liberty Bell, talked about her idyllic childhood. "There was always a whole herd of us kids going on hikes, pretending, building forts. I'll always have good memories of this place."

But even Michelle won't commit herself to living on the ranch.

"To come back here must be a step of strength, not of weakness," acknowledged Don Wallis, father of two college-aged boys. It takes a commitment, he explained, to a way of life rather than a running away from something else.

"I hope our kids someday come to the realization, after they've gone away to the city, that money isn't everything," Karen Shaffer said. "I just hope this place will be kept intact for them to come back to when they're ready."

But who will "they" be?

Several speculate that perhaps it won't be the second generation that will return, after all. It may be the third.

(February 1987)

Postscript

I was approached recently by Karen West, who is working on projects for the Shafer Museum in Winthrop. She said these sketches should be published in the interest of fleshing out the story of the Methow Valley.

So I dug them out from the drawer where they had lain for a dozen years, and as I reread them, I was – I'm not trying to toot my horn here – surprised at how readable they were, and somehow timely. Suddenly all those ranchers and cowboys and loggers and cooks and gamblers and moonshiners and hippies came clattering back to life. They had plenty to say about this community at the edge of the wilderness.

All together, these stories form a mosaic of a place far from any interstate; they paint a portrait of a sequestered valley decades ago, full of strong characters who spoke out about what it was like to make a living in this remoteness.

Many of the old-timers in these stories are dead, many of the concerns and issues are forgotten. What was vibrantly current is now ignored. But there are also many people who are still here, changing with the times, and some concerns never die.

Obviously, the valley has changed dramatically since these stories were first written. Few ranchers are herding their cattle before them into the tall bunch grass, no one's here to go down into the mines. But for many, this place is still a refuge from the crowded and frantic world beyond its mountainous borders, and the gold each seeks is of individual shape and hue.

This book is a quiet read for times when we need to remember that the human race still possesses at least a few redeeming qualities. It is for those who would care to plumb the depths of the place they've chosen to call home. There is still no doubt in my mind that this is a special place, even a sacred one. To recall and listen to those who have come before us is to add more texture to the fabric of our own lives.

I agree with Ronald Blythe, who wrote "Akenfield," a portrait of an English village, in 1969. He said, "I think my view of human life is how brief and curious most people's lives are. Yet when you come to talk to them you realize how strong they are and how unbelievably rich their lives are; also subtle and various."

Amen.

Diana Hottell
Twisp, Washington
(January 2007)

About the Author

Diana Hottell

Diana Hottell was born in Washington, D.C., in 1946, to Mildred Lee Watts, a direct descendant of "Light-Horse Harry" Lee (father of Gen. Robert E. Lee), and Philip Watts. Her father was in government service and Diana grew up in a household frequented by Cold War-era political luminaries.

She attended Catholic University for one year, then went to Greece to attend College Year in Athens. As a result, she speaks Greek – as well as French, German, Italian and Spanish, "all of them imperfectly," she says.

In 1966, she married Bill Hottell, a piano player and ex-Jesuit seminarian, who grew up in Spokane. He first came to Diana's attention when she heard piano music coming from the open window of a basement apartment three doors from her parents' home. "I liked him because he had a sense of adventure," she says.

The couple first lived in Southern California while Bill completed service in the U.S. Marine Corps. In 1968, they embarked on a 19-month tour, mostly by Volkswagen van, of Europe, Africa, Australia and the

Middle East, including today's geopolitical hot spots: Lebanon, Pakistan, Afghanistan, Iran and Iraq.

Afterwards, they perched briefly in New Orleans, where Bill taught in an all-black school, then moved to Ketchikan where Bill taught in an all-white school. At night, they played piano and banjo at Helen's Piano Bar, and earned a huge amount of money in tips, never declared. In 1971, the pair once again climbed aboard a Volkswagen van and began a year-long drive from Alaska to the southern tip of South America.

In 1972, just as the new North Cascades Highway was opening the Methow Valley to profound changes, the roaming adventurers came to roost near Twisp, next door to Ferry County, where Bill had spent his first few years.

Diana and Bill were immediate hits at the Antlers Tavern, where they played for the next 17 years. The Hottell Ragtime Jazz Band continues to have a devoted following.

In 1976, Mae Darwood, editor of the Methow Valley News, asked Diana, who had no training as a journalist, to profile valley residents for the newspaper. She spent the next 18 years writing about the Methow Valley and its people, the last nine of them for the Wenatchee World.

"When we moved to the valley, we had no idea we'd spend the next 35 years here. Little by little our lives have unfolded amazingly. It's been yet another adventure just being here," she says.

Solveig Torvik
Winthrop, Washington
(January 2007)